The Exposure of Anti Christ's League Of The Untouchables, Inc.

by
John Wesley Ellis

Bloomington, IN  Milton Keynes, UK

authorHOUSE™

AuthorHouse™
1663 Liberty Drive, Suite 200
Bloomington, IN 47403
www.authorhouse.com
Phone: 1-800-839-8640

AuthorHouse™ UK Ltd.
500 Avebury Boulevard
Central Milton Keynes, MK9 2BE
www.authorhouse.co.uk
Phone: 08001974150

First published by AuthorHouse 8/16/2006

ISBN: 1-4259-4111-7 (e)
ISBN: 1-4259-4110-9 (sc)
ISBN: 1-4259-1932-4 (dj)

Library of Congress Control Number: 2006904712

Printed in the United States of America
Bloomington, Indiana

This book is printed on acid-free paper.

Table of Contents

Chapter Eleven

Chapter Twelve

Introduction

There is a very great need to expose the works of the Antichrist, before he is in complete control of all of the deceived nations. The Saints of the Most High know that his dreadful course will only last for three-and-a-half years. Preparations for those who will repent during his reign will be necessary. This allegorical book will be a help to all of those who are left behind, because of being unworthy to be a part of that great-foreordained rapture. Places for shelter, food, water, raiment, medicine, and communication — unknown to the Antichrist — will be needed during this period. The Saints of God, presently, do not have the knowledge of those who will be left behind who God will have mercy on during the tribulation era. The Church can only make certain preparations that only God can make known to those that will repent after the rapture.

The metaphorical word, "untouchable," (used in the title of this book) is an expression of how the world has allowed Satan, the futuristically Antichrist, and the destruction demons, to take over and do as they please with almost no resistance at all. The pleasures of death now dominate the world. The influence of the hosts and hostesses of death has made its way into the houses of prayer. Instead of the people of God increasing unto the mark for the prize of the high calling of God in Christ Jesus, they are indulging in the things to profane the ways of Holiness.

Personally, I am ashamed of the ones whose eyes and ears have been deceived unto the point of being rejected. Why, oh man and woman, can you not see that your soul is being poisoned unto death? So many people of God are against the Truth, and the ways of Holiness, which is Life! The new, deadly, lustful combination spirit of the mockers has infiltrated their way into the places of worship. The mock lesbian pastor, the mock pedophile priest, and the mock gay bishop are noticeable acts of the outward functionality of this deadly spirit.

In this book, we will be monitoring the manifested acts of the Antichrist. This is the declaration of his will, which is to destroy and cause as many souls as possible to receive eternal damnation. I pray to God that you live to repent.

Chapter One
Meeting Minutes in the High Place

Chairman: We are here to discuss the destruction of a nation that has the potential to interfere with our plans to govern the world. We are also here to set in motion the defilements that would cause the wrath of God upon the rejected nations, especially the nations that protect Israel. The judges — our cunning secretaries — are doing a great job. The foundation laws of God are being removed; the headstrong women are taking over; the demonized men are marrying men; the silly women, who are laden with sins, are marrying women; the apostatized carnal congregations are falling into seduction; millions of mothers are murdering their unborn children; and we have fixed it so that our blinded priests can't have wives. Money is too valuable to take care of their wives and children, if we allowed them to get marry. Let them be a see if you can get away with it, pedophile. Thanks to the weak and blinded men and women, our evil techniques are not being detected. Master Mammon is so beloved that they would sell their soul, if it was detachable.

Master Mammon: I am currently working on a means to force the Christians to abandon their faith. By removing the present currency that is in the world, and demanding them to come to me, for an exchange of worshipping-to-buy program, we can and will be successful. Remember how Nebuchadnezzar had the fiery furnace built, that brought everyone under the submission of worshipping the golden image. The appearance of the fire changed their minds. We want to be more deceptive. A person must eat to live. In order to eat, someone must buy. A mark, just to buy, is not good enough to deceive and destroy. A worship, mark, and buy program will be necessary. The professed Christians do not know it, but it is the idolized worshipping of the image of the Beast that we are after, that will mark them forever. By worshipping the image of the Beast that we will be setting up, to live and deceive, we will bring the people into complete submission to our deadly cause. We must somehow establish a death sentence for non-compliance.

Judges: We want you to know that everything is going according to our plan. Before they realize what is taking place, it will be too late. We would not have a possible chance if they honored God's Laws. God's Laws are their protection. We had a hard time accomplishing their removal. Now everything is set. We soon will have a lawless nation that can be under our jurisdiction.

Chairman: My time is short, and I must make haste. My embodiment — of all of my evil and cunning ways — must be without detection. I always wanted to be in complete control and deified, but this time, it's revenge and deification! We will do all that we possibly can to cause man to destroy himself. Our mission is to destroy everything that God loves, and everything that he hates will be promoted to the highest order. Our progress, for our totalitarian government, is very good; but we must keep the pressure on the people to abolish their Christian Faith. The true Church is standing in our way. We would have been victorious a long time ago.

Vice President: The defilements that are being instituted by our seducing spirits is working. The God-given doctrine, for the Church, is being drastically changed. Master Mammon must make sure that our ministers have plenty of money to keep them motivated. When a lot of money is being allotted into their possession, the Truth is concealed and never revealed. They will please the people, and administer to them what they want to hear. They want to hear about the prospect of monetary gain and not repentance.

Chairman: You must find me the perfect body that I can fully work through without any hindrance or detection. I need a well-established position that the world already honors and respects that is for life without voting every few years. Whatsoever I do or say must be accepted with no questions asked. I have already experienced an embodiment that failed more than once. I need a God-fearing, infallibly-accepted body that can deceive the very elect. Master Mammon will supply you with the funds to make sure that everything is taken care of promptly.

Chapter Two
Vexed Beyond Measure

As Lot's soul was vexed, so is my soul, because it is very apparent that our nation, in general, has gone mad. The signs of purity and righteousness are very rare. Instead of producing the offspring of ladies and gentlemen, the matrix is bringing forth vessels for demonic embodiments. Why has there been such a drastic change in the minds of the people in this nation after so many good and blessed years? If the present trend continues, the next step will be a kingdom divided against itself, for the historical statistics of the rising and falling of a nation.

Why are you allowing so many major companies to just pack up and leave after becoming filthy rich through the hands of dedicated American citizens? Those responsible for being so greedy and leaving should be brought to court for being extremely unjust. Will we become a servant nation to the rest of the world? Will there be enough fast food chains and shopping malls in our country for the people to work? Will the wages be sufficient to sustain our present lifestyles? On the other hand, will there be nowhere to turn to but against each other? Where will the thousands of college graduates work? The economists should understand that what is taking place now means economic disaster in the future. We are being schemed out of our jobs for greed and cheaper labor. If you do not understand the Antichrist's plan, you need to find someone who does.

The men and women that are in this country do not have the right to bring this place into an act of abominations of sacred desecration that brings consequential desolation. You should be ashamed of yourselves for destroying the gift of God's given wisdom of mother wit. When cancer is in its malignant stage, there is very little hope for continuous longevity of earthly life. At the present rate of increasing evils, this nation will not persevere into the next century.

For the sake of the precious souls that Elohim has brought by birth into this sacred nation, there is a need to explore the unknown workings of our archenemy. The words that you are about to read are allegorical, for the sole purpose of letting you see just how cunning and evil Satan really is.

We now welcome you to Satan's New and Advanced Workshop. This workshop is so advanced that you would have to be the pure in heart, with God's anointing, to uncover the deceiving operations for people and especially to corrupt the Church. Let us begin in this area, which is the Call Girl Studio. Here, in this studio, we give women the mind and the means to look sexy. We also design the apparels and jewelry called SexWear, for lust that they can wear to tease men and drive them crazy. Even though a woman might be a virgin or a chaste wife, we still have the knowledge of how to make her look unclean and help us to destroy a weak brother's mind and his pure thoughts. We have the knowledge of how to get the women who go to church to interfere with Sunday morning services. We give them the unknowingly ability to come looking to appeal and not to worship. Who do you think invented the long, bird-claw, dipping nails that women think look so pretty? We have managed to filter in the acceptance of pants and shorts that women wear when they attend church services. The women are the easiest ones to work with, because their minds are very vulnerable in the area of perception. When a woman is given an implant of desires, only the power of God can break her. If the power of God does not intervene, we will continually have a multitude of vessels for our causes.

In this next area, we have the Music of Us Bands. Here we manufacture all of the sounds for the music that God hates. We also recruit spiritual singers into our bands, because the pay is much greater. We take our new mixer and blend in the demonic music with the church music. The youth just love it. We now have the rappers, the break-dancers, and the ballet performers, working for us to corrupt the churches. They use to work in their field or in certain areas only, but now the churches just are overwhelmed with this type of entertainment. You see those tanks over there? They are filled with laughing spirits. These spirits take the minds away from being sincere and make the Word of God to be humorously funny. Our latest employees are called the Laughing

Profaners, which are responsible for the distribution of these spirits.

We are now in the room called the High Place, which is the most deadly place in existence. Here in this place, the operations for eternal damnation are discussed. Satan and all of his associates come here. Not too long ago, they made plans to remove the Laws of God from a certain nation's judicial system. Moreover, guess what, it happening? Man, they were using Black Magic and everything else, but to no avail. But when they decided to demonize nine of their top officials, they were successful. I do not know what is going to happen to that nation, but Satan is out for elimination. This is the sad part. It was so sad, that if I were not a demon, I would be crying and mourning myself. Out of all of inhabitants of that nation, the resistance was almost as nothing. It was a walk-right-in-and –sit-right-down move!

For our entertainment, we watch the Darwin Show. We watch the highly-educated men and women dig into the rocks and the earth to find out what really happened — they say — billions of years ago. This is the humorous part. When they find a bone, or a group of bones, they rejoice. Little do they know that the substances of the tools that they were digging with are older than the bones that they found. After their findings, they begin to imagine all kinds of theories, and from theories, they move into lies. We may be demons but we are not that dumb. These men and women went to school to become unintelligent, because they have concluded— by digging in the rocks —that there is no God.

Now, we have to hoodwink you to take you to the oldest and greatest place of our deceiving operations. We did not make any changes whatsoever to this facility. Behold, the Lucifer Institution of Disobedience. Our motto is "It is better to obey us than to obey God." Every soul, whose name is not in the Lamb's Book of Life, has been here. The uniqueness of this facility is that you do not have to be present in our classroom to learn how to be disobedient. We have a special, patented way to summon our students' minds here for instructions. The richest of the richest were here. The minds of the most evil men on earth have been here. Preachers who were once obedient ended up here. They became dropouts from that other school because of women and money. We cannot disclose the names of our current mind/body, because of our Privacy

Act. However, if you are wise enough, you will understand by the reaction of those who have been attending this institution.

Is there a reason why I wrote this allegory? Yes, indeed! People are suffering greatly because the citizens of this world have refused to summit themselves unto the will of God. They have chosen death, of whom they think is so pretty, rich, and famous. Nevertheless, when he is finished with you, at the time of graduation, he will give you a degree to be set at 212 degrees Fahrenheit or more. He will welcome you into his domain. He will congratulate you, and give you a job of weeping, gnashing of the teeth, embedded in worms that will not die, in darkness, without a drop of water, and without ever being unemployed again. Thank you for going to the school of your choice.

Chapter Three
The Jurisdiction of Totalitarianism Under the Antichrist

Some time ago, a woman's husband decided that her feeding tube should be removed. He subsequently caused her to starve to death without any mercy whatsoever. A society with over 250 million people, a helpless judicial system, and a weak, feebleminded police force could not stop the act of the words that proceeded out of the mouth of one man.

For over 200 years, the Ten Commandments were highly honored and respected, and were the foundation for every righteous law that was made in this nation. The Antichrist, through his antichrists, is now saying that they are unconstitutional, and must be removed and displayed like a monument on the outside, which is a prominent sign of rejection. God's law is our freedom; and if it is now just a monument, then catastrophically violence and wickedness stands at the door. Until there is an unconditional, complete surrendering of the fact that God's law is our freedom, and until they are restored back into the original status of how our founding forefathers honored them, this nation will suffer greatly at the hands of the Almighty God.

Evil, supernatural totalitarianism, in its essence, is the inability to govern and think for yourself. Satan will rule this world for a short period of time through his deceptive appointee. The infestation of innumerable micro-demons will be deployed at that time. Without the divine sealing of Elohim, everyone else will be susceptible to demonic obedience, and sequentially, will become Satan's reprobated, evil mutants.

Is the door to God's great Grace shut? If this is so, then someone is now in a hopeless state. If the door is shut unto the Gentiles, then it is open unto the house of David. Warnings upon warnings were made known to the Gentiles to repent and turn from wickedness, but so many have given Elohim a deaf ear. Evil will come to an end, and all of those who are a part of it. Sin is not beautiful, and abominations are not pretty.

When two men are involved in a shootout over a piece of chicken — leaving one dead — evil supernaturalism is taking place. When a married mother decides to murder — and aborts her healthy fetus of 5 months — evil supernaturalism is taking place. When two grown men, weighing 200 pounds each, fall in love and get married, and perform the act of making children to each other — who don't have the knowledge of the difference between a pond and a sewer — evil supernaturalism is taking place. When a man kills another man for his car rims (that when driving, he cannot see on his car), evil supernaturalism is taking place. All of the evil acts of abnormality that are now taking place in our world are the works of evil, supernaturally-influenced totalitarianism. The proclaimed satanic reward for a suicide bomber, to rid the world of infidels, is continuous virginal intercourses in paradise with seventy women. Wouldn't it be wiser for Elohim to just shut up the matrix and let natural causing death have its course? The idiotic proclamation — to kill for sex — came from the pits of Hell, and is a cunning, deceitful means to recruit bodies for evil, supernatural totalitarian acts.

Chapter Four
Truth Court II

Case Name: Freedom as is: The Spirits of our Founding Forefathers and the Voices of the Truth vs. The Supreme Court

Plaintiff: Our Founding Forefathers

Defendant: All of the Judges who voted to have the Ten Commandments removed

Plaintiff: Oh ye unrighteous judges, how long shall God's great Grace watch over you to keep you from destroying yourselves? I sincerely ask you this question. Do you realize what you have done? The Constitution is a God-given gift for our unique freedom, and above all things, it was created to protect the Church upon which the contents of is based. Secular intuitional minds, nor the sole might of men, had nothing to do with the establishment of this sacred nation. The hundreds of years of intellectual heightening cannot change this cornerstone-laid foundation. From our graves, we will contend with you until you come to your senses and the knowledge of the Truth. Not only must the Ten Commandments be restored back to its original status for our protection, but must be honored above every other existing laws in our judicial system.

Defendant: How in the world are you going to come against us in your graves? We are in the twenty-first century with the power to judge as we see fit. When this country was being established, sure, all of the people were predominantly Christians, but now we must consider the beliefs of all of the other ethnic groups. Therefore, we must be universal in judgments, and completely disconnect our governmental functions from any one said religion. The incorporation of religious beliefs into our government was good in its time, but today — because of our interrelationships with other countries — we must refrain from openly-religiously-influenced statements that cause tension.

Plaintiff: First, it is the precious gift of God for preservation that will come up against you, which is in the hearts of the people who love and cherish this freedom of the Free Indeed. Our God-given wisdom and purity, for the establishment of this great nation, will bring you down from self-exaltation to humble submission. Your impaired judgments are being influenced by the telepathic surreptitious words of the Antichrist. A judgment that puts our nation into an even-greater vulnerable state is unconstitutional. This nation does not need anyone from any ethnical group here to cause a denouncement of our foundational Christian heritage. If the words and the laws of the one and only true and living God is offensive, then let them return to their own country, where the same God is being rejected for a piece of stone or wood, and for man-made apostatized doctrines. The truthful Word of God is the foundation of our profound and secured freedom.

Defendant: The judgments that are now being made are for the people. The people want to promote secularism, and as it is stated, "we the people," we must comply.

Plaintiff: Which group of people are you referring to in this country? Every Satanic-made religion, or no belief at all, is a part of secularism. Satan has taught his devoted subjects to use the word "religion" for operational concealments, tax exempt status, and deceitful recruitment. When supernatural totalitarianism is influencing you to denounce your faith-based heritage, your judgments are for the Antichrist's cause, and no one else's. A judgment for the security and well-being of the people is far greater than any emotional satisfaction of the ears. Any religion that has a directive to rid the world of infidels through senseless terrorism is under the influence of the Antichrist. The infidels need God's Grace. Our true and living God will judge every man accordingly for his works. The earful lying words of compensation, for an unlawful, degrading, psychoactive, suicide bomber, came from the workings of the Antichrist. The sacred laws of freedom and tranquility must be restored.

Defendant: Our financial market in this country consists of people from all over the world, and we must respect their beliefs. We cannot afford to let the passed interpretations of our Constitution interfere with the present. The predominantly Christian epical status is a thing of the pass.

Plaintiff: Are we hearing you all right? You mean to tell us that the financial status of this nation is greater than its security and protection?

Will you also sell our God-given freedom for a dollar? Did Master Mammon set you up for his own evil devices? What is your compensation for having our protection removed?

Defendant: Secularism is for our future new world order that will bring harmony and stability into our world. We must comply with the needs of the people. We will make new laws that constitute peace and safety.

Plaintiff: The laws that are now being made to govern this country are for our destruction and elimination. Satan wants this nation to be destroyed and powerless, because we are a threat to his future regime. Satan is out to destroy Christianity and you are his puppets. Christianity is not just the only true religion in this world, but is our utmost profound protection from the forces of evil. You have already passed a law that gave the mothers in this country the right to destroy millions of Elohim's to-be children. Now, you are trying to pass a law that would destroy our freedom. The laws for abortion rights are for stealthy depopulation. Adolph Hitler was an openly-manifested genocidal dictator. The abortionists, in today's world, are sophisticated, doctoral, legal, and inhumane licensed by the judicial system, genocidal butchers of the unborn. The abortionists are not only just butchers, but are typical modern-day Doctor Jekyll and Mister Hydes being compensated for murderous acts against humanity and Heaven. The laws for homosexuality are for depopulation, wrathful destruction, and futuristic elimination. The unnoticed industrial migration is for chaos. After you realize that millions of jobless people will need financial assistance, your eyes will come open. Master Mammon is also Satan's certified demonic accountant. He is secretly using the CEOs in this country to transfer funds and businesses into the region where the Antichrist will be establishing his totalitarian government. Sins and abominations increase diseases which cause death. It is hard for an unruly child to become a good soldier. Look at your young men on the streets and tell us who will be in your army in the time of war in the future? Ask yourselves this question: Are the judgments which you are making for the prospect of God's wrath upon us? The doctrine of a certain extremist religion has neither grace, nor mercy for another human being outside of his or her demonic occult. There is no freedom in a lied-to-based nation. Furthermore, there are those now present in this country who can become your enemies because of religious beliefs and what is being done in their country. Their beliefs are weapons for destruction and elimination. The Truth of the Kingdom of God, that no one can stop or destroy, will soon dominate the world and bring eternal peace and joy. Amen. WE REST OUR CASE.

The Deliberation and Verdict of the Divine Electoral Timed Jurors: We have watched, very closely, the changes that this nation has made from its sacred foundation until this present time. We watched how the women changed their clothing from the down-to-the-ankle apparel to the string bikinis. We watched the mothers of dear children change from motherhood to aborting murderhood. We watched the people of peace and safety change to vicious criminals. We watched the laws of righteousness changed into the laws of devils. We watched the desecration of sacred prayer in the schools for the acceptance of secularism. We watched how morals were rejected for immorality. We watched the families of old be dismantled by the judicial system. We watched the greedy get greedier. We watched the embodying of demons that caused men and women to alter their existing gender. We watched the demons that caused the burning desires of lust for reprobated homosexuality. The present chaotic state of this nation is mainly based on the laws that you have made. Millions of Elohim's children would have existed to fulfill their earthy course of life, just as you did, if you would have judged justly. You did not become a Supreme Court justice through an unwise mother, who decided to abort her fetus. Nor did you come into this world through a sewer, but a matrix. Why did you make such an inhuman decision to pollute this nation with innocent bloodshed? Did not you read your Holy Bibles? God destroyed Sodom and Gomorrah for the same immoral conduct of men today, and your judgments are helping them to become a repeated factor of this same-like-unto outcome. The security and protection of this nation is based upon the revealed Truth that was given unto your ancestors. According to the Divine Omniscient Laws of Elohim, you are GUILTY! There is no freedom in secularism. Secularism is Satanic lied-to totalitarianism. We the jury, do hereby find the defendant guilty of treason to the highest degree. By a unanimous vote, on all charges, we concluded that you have been an aid to the now-present condition of this country. You knowingly dishonored the true statues that were set forth by your founding ancestors, and chose to side yourselves with the forces of evil, and passed laws against God and the blessed inhabitants in this nation.

Because of God's infinite wisdom and great Grace, we, the jury, request that the defendants be granted seven years to mend their ways and to repent, and restore back the things which they have cause to be destroyed. If, after seven years, the defendant will not comply with the ruling of this court, the presiding Omnipotent Righteous Judge will sentence you according for your deeds.

Case Name: Antichrist's Daughter

The Voices of the Truth vs. the Puppet Mind of Antichrist's Bewitched Daughter

Plaintiff: The Helpless Minds of Innocent Children and the Voices of the Truth

Defendant: The Merciless Daughter of the Antichrist

Plaintiff: Oh woman of all subtlety, whose mind is engrafted with every art of magic and witchcraft working to destroy the minds of helpless innocent children, for the only cause of compensating riches, being paid to you by Master Mammon. You were made from the rib of a man to help and assist him in this world. Master Mammon has employed and blinded you for the very cause of the destruction of our minds. Why did you choose the art of magic and witchcraft to write in your published books, and instill within our minds that we can do and become likewise, to venture into real evil Black Magic. We are young, helpless-minded children trying to learn how to grow up and be good men and women. How are we going to be good from what you are teaching us? In our youth, the principals for righteousness must be instilled within us, not how to become sorcerers and witches. Can you fully understand that this knowledge of magic and witchcraft is detrimental even for adults? Will our minds be sensed to cast spells upon those who we dislike or disapprove? What morals are you teaching us? Are you really trying to teach us how to read or are you making us to be the servants for the Antichrist in the future? What knowledge of resistance of evil do we have? Will we be able to become pure-minded Christians? Alternatively, are we all doomed to hell and destruction? Will we live a long life? Will we be able to obey our parents? How can we play with the other kids with such an infatuated mind? Are we Antichrist's new recruitments? Admit your guilt. You are laying the groundwork for Antichrist's acceptance. You know right well that the Antichrist will be using Black Magic and Witchcraft to deceive the people, and to establish a deadly, false religion with great signs and wonders. It is better to be illiterate than to become a servant of sorcery and witchcraft. What will be your epitaph after you are deceased? Will it be "the woman who the Antichrist used to destroy the minds of helpless children?" What will you tell Jesus Christ when you stand before him in judgment? Will you tell him that you were only trying to help them learn how to read from something that would interest the mind? Alternatively, will you tell him the truth, which is the preparation of the young and the helpless for the workings of the Antichrist? Why do not you just repent of this great evil, and teach the children how to love God, honor his son, Jesus Christ, and to obey their parents? You are rich enough already for being a merciless instrument to help destroy the minds of helpless children. Oh, woman, you are in great trouble! We rest our case.

The defendant was not allowed to speak in this case. Her own mind was inoperative at that time. Any group of words that would have proceeded out of her mouth will not be her own words. She died a spiritual death a long time ago, with a very little hope in sight.

The Deliberation and Verdict of the Divine Electoral Timed Jurors: Because of the inability to be merciful and caring for helpless children; having the knowledge of what is right in the sight of God; choosing to gain earthly riches over the preservation of precious souls; we the jury do hereby find you guilty of mindslaughter! You are doubling guilty for working against Elohim. Those children who you are helping to destroy belong to Elohim! He did not bring them into this world to be destroyed but for salvation! Your agenda is one of greed and nothing else, at the expense of helpless children! We are requesting that the Righteous Judge give you a just sentencing accordingly for your evil works!

THE CARING VOICE OF AN ANONYMOUS SOUL: WOMAN, PLEASE FOR THE SAKE OF THE LOVE FOR HUMANITY, REPENT!

Sentencing: The sentencing is pending until she repents or is finally deceased, blessed for repentance and cursed for a continuation of evil works.

Case Name: Deceived out of Grace

The True Givers of Jesus Christ vs. the Tithe Demons

Plaintiff: The True Cheerful Givers and the Voices of the Truth

Defendant: The Tithe Demons and their Associates

The Tithe Demons: For what cause have we been summoned to this court? We have been so faithful in our operations. We have supported the church and the poor, in acquiring sufficient funds to meet all of the needs of the people. We make sure that everyone in the church is happy.

The True Cheerful Givers: Why are you lying to this court? This is the Truth Court, where only the disclosures of the truth are made. You must speak the Truth!

The Tithe Demons: Well, the truth is that our job is to provide our ministers with a lot of money, so that they can deceive and be deceived out of the realm of God's Grace. From our satanic teachings, we found out that vast amounts of money could change people for the worse. We deceive by causing people to think that they are blessed. Nevertheless, the truth is that they are delusively blessed. People will do many unjust things to maintain their status of well-being. Master Mammon has conditioned our ministers outlandishly, so that they will not tell people the truth. The desire for money works for us. Did you think for one moment, that we would be making our ministers rich if they were telling the truth? No! We would be trying to destroy them, just like in the days of old.

Who do you think started the filling out of applications for membership, and the financial disclosures of those desiring to be a part of certain congregations? It definitely was not the Holy Spirit. Who do you think send the deacons to the members' houses to enforce the promised tithes of certain congregations? Who do you think established the "if-you-do-not-pay" ordinances or convinced you that you would be expelled if you failed to pay? Our recent programs are so unique. It is much more about entertainment than salvation. By keeping our ministers' pockets lined and filled, our part becomes very easy. We teach our servants to refrain from rebuking the people for committing sin. Our motto is that a happy soul gives more than a rebuked individual.

With the new programs in place, we finance the rappers of the gospel, the incorporated ballet dancers and break-dancers of praise teams, and the new contemporary gospel. We love the gospel rock that our ministers bring into the mega churches for the young people. The hip-hop music is great.

The True Cheerful Givers: Why did you lie about helping the poor? You had better tell us the absolute truth without any deception in mind!

The Tithe Demons: The truth is that people who are not so well-off and poor are the ones who have the greatest opportunity of entering into God's kingdom. Their minds are clearer and not polluted with great desires. When you are rich, that man or woman becomes a statistical self-righteous justifier. Although our operations are church related, the people love to idolize rich people. Regardless of what they do or say, the more that you have, the greater you are. You can get married ten times, have a dozen affairs, get buck naked before the people, and become a homosexual or a lesbian, the people will only look at what you can do and how much money do you have. They will never cease to glorify that person. They will even idolize the clothes that they wore after they are deceased.

We do not want to disclose any more information of our secret operations to this court. It hurts us greatly to tell you the truth. We know that you will eventually share this knowledge with the whole world, and try to defeat us. Nevertheless, we have a stronghold in the world that will never end.

Everything in existence belongs to God. However, riches are obtained in two very different ways. Our way is the best way. Goodness and mercy is excluded from all of our operations. Why do you think that we are called the Tithe Demons? The poor and needy are not on our list to be helped. We do our very best to take what little they do have and give it to our servants. Again, who do you think started the hundred dollar and fifty dollar prayer lines in certain services in the places of worshipping? Who do you think is the author of Purgatory? If money could get us back to the place where we were thrown out of, we would not have any problems whatsoever.

Our servants have gold faucets, diamond rings, mansions, airplanes, the best clothes and shoes, and the best cars in the world. We make the poor and needy think that they must have these things to worship and do God's business. We do not want to say this, but the truth is the truth. Jesus Christ of Nazareth possessed only his clothes on his back and shoes on his feet while here on earth. After everything that he did to help man, they gambled over his seamless garment that he wore. He was victorious over the works of the devil, without the appearance of greatness. He used the Love of God to establish his father's kingdom that has no end. We definitely should not be disclosing this, what we are about to say. We would be ashamed of what is taking place in the churches of today if we were still in heaven. The people are so weak that they will idolize a piece of toast that has an image of someone.

If our ministers would care for the poor and needy, they would be broke. It takes a lot of money to deceive people. The only other way, which we can care less about, is God's way of obtaining riches. Through the Omniscient will of God, for the good and well-being of all humanity, he will grant certain men and women riches and with the wisdom to have them. With his great Grace, he will keep them humbly in his care.

The True Cheerful Givers: Why are you still lying to us? You know right well that you do not have a stronghold on your operations that will never end! Your end is near and you know it, for you and your associates.

The Associates of the Tithe Demons: We have not done anything wrong. We have accumulated a few extra dollars for ourselves because the people are concerned about our well-being. We may have many expensive things, because we deserve the best, and our goals are to reach as many individuals as possible. People love greatness. Why did the Jews reject their Messiah? He came in the low estate of a common man. Nowadays, it does not work either. To reach people, you need money and a lot of it. Salvation is free, but the airways and the telecasts used to declare the Gospel are costly. When Jesus Christ was here, the earthly population was not as great as it is today. We enforce tithe-giving because there is a need. If we do not enforce tithe- giving, then we are going to be out of business. Once we are out of business, then the world is going to be in great trouble. We are helping to keep the

Antichrist at bay. We do not have anything to do with these so-called Tithe Demons.

The True Cheerful Givers: You have spoken well. You do not have anything to do with the Tithe Demons. The truth is that they have something to do with you. The Tithe Demons stated earlier, that their mission is to deceive you and in turn help you to deceive others, so that both parties are out of the realm of God's Grace. The truth is the greatest force in existence. Now we will hear the truth of the whole matter.

The Voices of the Truth: The Antichrist is strengthened through deceptions. The more individuals that he deceives, the stronger he becomes. The kingdoms of this world are falling into his hands. The people are being blinded beyond measure. Although the scriptures must be fulfilled, there will always be a church without a spot or wrinkle, or any such thing. Someone's feet will always be beautiful that preach the gospel of peace and bring glad tidings of good things. Someone will preach the same identical gospel that Peter and the rest of the apostles preached. Someone will always be pressing toward the mark for the prize of the high calling of God in Christ Jesus. Someone will never yield to the things that the Antichrist has established for his kingdom. Someone will be doing their very best to keep the Antichrist from corrupting and polluting God's house. They will keep the rappers of the gospel, the demonic music, the break-dancers, the ballet performers, and everything else out of God's house that is ungodly and unholy. Someone will not put the poor and needy in a state that would diminish what little he or she does have. Someone will have the heart and the Holy Spirit to be merciful. Someone will continue to teach the aged men to be sober, that they might teach the young men of today how to be a gentleman — and also how to pull up their pants that people will not see their next-to-shame garments. Someone will teach the aged women how to be an example for the young women, that they may teach them that it is despicable to wear skintight pants. Those women who wear such garments become the agents who produce the thoughts of evil desires. Someone will teach sound doctrine, that the aged women will also teach the young women not to present themselves as being whorish and a web to lure men's thoughts into intimate desires. What shall we say? Shall we praise you? Apparently, the ministers who are not performing all of these things for the promotion of God's kingdom are not those who we are referring.WE REST OUR CASE.

The Deliberation and Verdict of the Divine Electoral Timed Jurors: Why did you let the demons deceive you? For what reason are all of these changes taking place in the churches? How can you be justified in your present state? Is this how you show God that you love him? You have not even come close to fulfilling "thy will be done in earth as it is in heaven." You have allowed the places of worship to become entertainment centers instead of the houses of prayer.

Your voices are that of an investment broker, trying to make a sales pitch for earthly gain, telling the people that God will heal the land and your money. Why cannot you speak the same words that the apostles spoke? Your eyes are sick and your tongues are afraid to tell the people the Truth. In your hearts, you say, "If I tell them the truth, I would lose lots of money." Sirs, what about the souls that are sincerely in need of the truth? Are you right for holding the words that can save people from death and hell? Open your eyes and not your wallets. Look at the women of whom you have the oversight. Do they look like holy women who can stand before the omnipresence of Jesus Christ? With the dresses so short, sitting on the front row, revealing the color of their intimate garments, how are you going to tell this court that you are innocent? Refusing to tell the men that earrings represent femininity, how are you going to tell us that you are innocent? Taking the Word of God and using it comedically to entertain people, how can you be innocent? Did Jesus Christ of Nazareth suffer and die for this kind of behavior? Is this the holiness that the Apostle Paul spoke of, saying, "Follow peace with all men, and holiness without which no man shall see the Lord." What you have allowed to take place in God's houses of prayer are the works of the Antichrist. The Antichrist and Master Mammon have corrupted your minds by causing you to help corrupt and destroy the souls of many men and women. The Holy Spirit is so grieved because of your contemporary ways. Are you really going to continually be accessories of the Antichrist and lose your souls? For now, this jury hereby finds you sick and in need of that great physician, Christ Jesus. In seven years, you will be summoned again. You now have a great opportunity to mend your ways. We found that it was necessary to grant you God's Grace, because you were deceived. Now you know the Truth. The reason why the Tithe Demons were summoned was that they are the very ones that caused the deceptions. They can never be innocent. YE MEN OF GOD, GO YOUR WAY AND BE NOT ENTANGLED AGAIN WITH THESE DEMONS.

Chapter Five
The Abuse of Grace

Just the other day, at a place of worshipping, the sense for seeing was filled with indignant disgrace! The women were so loose that illusive tempting was their main objective. They had no conscious respect at all for the house of prayer. They had on party dresses with the kitchen greatly exposed. Their minds were geared for outward adorning and not for a spiritual cause that would help the soul. Instead, they were Satan's assistants, with distractions to make the Word of God less effective. This contemporary generation of many women has abandoned shamefacedness and has chosen the attire of disdaining harlots.

The house for worshipping is becoming more like a nightclub. The Word of God is now having a very little affect on the lives of many people. They are coming to God's house to be entertained and for socializing. The music that is being played in many sanctuaries is no difference than that which is played in the nightclubs. The recording artists, who are categorically called Rhythm and Blues Artists, sing in churches and nightclubs. The words in their songs are written to entertain both groups, without the word God or Jesus Christ. They enjoy the revenue coming from the Christians and non-Christians. The ballet industry has now taken up residence in the apostatized congregations. They are tiptoeing through the tulips before the people, in close-to-being-underwear garments, on the most sacred place in the building. While the angels of the churches are being amused on how they have managed to bring the young people into God's house, with entertainment and everything else they so desire, God is very displeased!

The noticeable concept, of the abuse of Grace, is summed up in these few words. Do all that you can if you think that you can get away with it and still be able to receive a crown of life from God in heaven after death. In short, form, Lord, let me know what all that I can do and still be saved. Why are you so easily deceived?

You have a mind to continue in sin, because someone has proclaimed that there is a place of purification after you are deceased. Sirs and madams, let me tell you the truth: Purgatory is an incentive not to be conscious of committing sin. Is this the reason why there are many professed priests who are pedophiles, because there is the presumption of there being a Purgatory? Whether you understand it or not, purification begins with repentance.

God's Great Grace is for repentance. There is no application of Grace without repentance. If you continue in sin, how can there be a true repentance? Repentance, in essence, is the turning away from sin and to be changed from darkness into light. How can a man be in the Light of Holiness and in darkness at the same time? Said words of being under Grace do not mean that you are a partaker of it. Grace is manifested when you fully repent. How can someone have the courage to stand before God and his people just after committing sodomy with a child? If there is no fear, there is no Grace for that man. If the same act reoccurs repeatedly, you are a part of reprobation. Reprobation is an act of Elohim, which is without Grace.

The abuse of Grace is an ever-more-manifested factor amongst those professing to be under the blood of Jesus Christ. Those who have said that they have put on Christ have adopted the ways and customs of the world. There is Great Grace for those who are under it, but no Grace for those who abuse it. Since the Lord our God is so merciful, so forgiving, and so loving, many people have come to the conclusion that regardless of what they do, the end of them is God's Grace. They have determined that hell is for the unbeliever. Grace is really for those who do not have an intent to sin or do wrong, but are under the influence of Satan.

When the Saints of God go to the gambling casinos and gamble, they are abusing Grace. The name of the Church, where you are a member, cannot be a means of your salvation without a righteous life. Because you were baptized as an infant does not mean that you can inherit an eternal life without Holiness. Tithes and offerings will not be accepted in exchange for ungodly living. Repentance is the beginning for obtaining God's Great Grace through Jesus Christ. You cannot be under Grace and still sin. Confession is invalid if it is your intent to commit that same sin again. Purgatory was invented for those who are sinful for an imaginary hope of enter into God's Kingdom. In plain and simple language, it is to make them feel good in knowing — they think — that they will eventually end up in Heaven.

Praying to Mother Mary so that she can pray to Jesus Christ for the forgiveness of sins is not a part of the New Covenant. Repentance and the forgiveness of sins through Jesus Christ of Nazareth is the foundation of the New Covenant. God has made two covenants with man. There is no such agreement in existence called a Second Hand Covenant. The Covenant of Catholicism was not ordained by Elohim, but by man. When Jesus Christ of Nazareth said, "That it is finished," that is exactly what he meant. The Old Covenant ended and the New Covenant was being signed with the precious blood of Jesus Christ into existence. God will not allow anyone to interpolate one jot or one title of this agreement. The New Covenant has been signed and sealed, so that it is impossible to be broken. Then who are you who think that they have the authority to change the doctrine of the New Covenant?

Who told you that you could not have a wife? God, Jesus Christ, the Holy Spirit — and anyone else who is of God — would never tell a man that he could not have a wife unless he was ordained for a special divine mission. Whosoever made the decree that the bishops could not marry was giving heed to seducing spirits and doctrines of devils. Furthermore, the man who made that decree is responsible for one of the reasons for the epidemic of the abuse of Grace. Who allowed you to be a proclaimed priest who is a pedophile? By Divine Definition, a pedophile is a reprobated crook and a felon. In order for a crook to be under God's Grace, he must first repent.

The apparel of Holiness will not make you innocent. The Eucharist is for those who are worthy, and damnable to everyone who is unworthy. How can you administer Holy Communion in the presence of the Almighty God to people without repentance? Instead of forgiveness and blessings, you are doing more harm than good. Homosexuals cannot have communion with Elohim. Murderers cannot have communion with God. Adulterers cannot have communion with God. Lesbians cannot have communion with God. Fornicators cannot have communion with God. Thieves and robbers cannot have communion with God. Shall I continue? You must repent before you can be in communion with the Lord Our God. Even a liar cannot tarry in his sight.

Why do men and women hate repentance? Someone is trying to find a doorway to escape repentance, because it means to stop sinning. Baptism and Grace is incomplete without repentance. You should be praying to stop sinning instead of trying to find someone to pray to God for your sins. Your prayers are heard when you decide in your heart to repent and give your life to Jesus Christ. You only need Jesus Christ of Nazareth to intercede on your behalf. Baptism is an act of obedience of the outward public confession of repentance. When a person is baptized, he or she is being cleansed for the remission of sin to receive the gift of the Holy Spirit. If you are being baptized for any other reason, it is invalid.

Infant baptism is good, as long as that person continues a life in Christ Jesus until death. In the early church, the whole family was baptized after they believed and accepted Christ. If you were baptized in your infancy, and you became an evil person in your adulthood, that infant baptism lost its status; because there was a breach of negligence, after becoming conscious in your adulthood, that you were baptized to live for Christ. You must repent and be baptized again in the name of Jesus Christ of Nazareth for the remission of sin! If you are so certain that you are still under Grace, then why are you still sinning?

Being under the power of God's Great, Manifested Grace means that you are under the direction of the Holy Spirit to fulfill his Divine Will. Millions have professed to be under the power of Grace, but are not. Someone proclaimed a doctrinal dogmatic group of words that would allow people to believe, be baptized, and — in sequence — be under the power of Grace. After the rituals, that person feels that he or she can do as they please without any repercussions, because of the possibility of being under the power of Grace. The power of Grace would never lead a person into the realm of wickedness and abominations. If certain professed bishops and priests were under the power of God's Grace, they would have been husbands instead of being pedophiles and rapists. If certain ones of the Sister Order were under the power of Grace, they would have shared the Grace that God gave them with Elohim's children that they destroyed. God would never lead a man or woman (who is under his guidance) into a state that he could not keep them. It is far better to be the least of all with a wife and many children than to be a pedophile who is about to enter into eternal damnation. It is far better to be a repented whore who spared their children, than to be a murderer who destroyed her offspring.

Oh man and woman, you are being deceived. The philosophy of dogmatism, concerning the doctrine of man's said grace, has a great risk factor. Can the words of man supersede the Word of God? It is written, that if the righteous scarcely be saved, where shall the ungodly and the sinner appear? There is no hope for those who have accepted dogmatism over the sound absolute doctrine of the New Covenant. If dogmatism is accepted as absolute, then how can absolute be dogmatic? If you think that you are under the power of Grace, then where is your witness? Grace begot Holiness for mankind and Holiness is the manifestation of Grace.

STOP ABUSING GRACE AND BECOME A PART OF IT, AND LET THE LIGHT OF GOD'S GRACE SHINE THROUGHOUT THE WHOLE WORLD. AMEN.

Chapter Six
The Last Love Letter

Freedom, my beloved sister, came to me and laid her head upon my breast. She asked me, with her Niagara tears, to help her, because she said "I am terminally ill and only have a very short time to live. My husband, Mr. Preambalo, said that he loves me and will never forsake me. After being faithful for over 200 years, he has decided to give me a bill of divorce. He wants to marry Secularia and Evolucy! Secularia can never be faithful, because she has no faith. She is atheistic. Evolucy is a liar and she will never tell you the whole truth. Secularia's name means lawlessness and abominations without end. Evolucy's name means someone who is ignorant. I am dying from a rare condition called Malignant Rejected Functionalism Failure. I am also heartbroken to the point of a non-repairable state. I am clean and pure. I wash myself every day with the Laws of God, and I use the best perfume in the world. I use the Scent of Truth. I clothe myself with wisdom and understanding. My feet are prepared for being compassionate and merciful. I will give my life for the Church and Mr. Preambalo. I never had in my mind of getting a divorce! Secularia and Evolucy are FILTHY and VERY EVIL! Their cholesterol count is in the millions, from all of those unborn fetuses that they have been trying to digest. Both of them have the Issue of Blood that no man can stop. It is the size of a river! Both of them have AIDS from messing around with Homo Polygamo Demontriel and Lesbiana Losforever. They will never be faithful! One of them is a so-called teacher. She is a mind-slaughterer of children. She is trying to teach them that they use to be like an ape. Listen to me very carefully: Secularia and Evolucy are working undercover for the Antichrist. He wants to make my husband get his divorce, and then he is going to assassinate him. Then he is going to marry Secularia and Evolucy. As long as I am alive, I am not going to forsake the True Church. God united Mr. Preambalo and me together for that sole reason of protecting the Church that Jesus Christ of Nazareth built. After the divorcement is completed, I am going to die! Secularia and Evolucy will marry Mr. Preambalo. All of the riches, glory, and honor will be in their possessions. The Antichrist will have Mr. Preambalo put to death. The Antichrist, Secularia, and Evolucy will inherit the riches from all of those years of hard labor. They will be merciless. I have emptied my heart out to you! PLEASE HELP ME!"

My beloved sister, hear me and hear me well. Elohim loves you and he will never forsake you. Mr. Preambalo did not only plan to reject you, but God as well. They crucified the Laws of God from their judicial system, and released the spirits of Secularia and Evolucy into the minds of the people. It is impossible for me to help you at this time, because you must fulfill the written prophesies of old. For three and a half years you must die to non-functionality. After that time, our Lord and Savior Jesus Christ will resurrect you. Your ringing will be heard in every country except Mystery Babylon the Great. You will rejoice with the Saints of the Most High God. Your name will be changed to FREE INDEED!

My dear brother, there are more things that I must tell you before I die! After my death, my children are going to be under the jurisdiction of the Antichrist and their stepmothers, Secularia and Evolucy. I believe that they are going to put Voteria in jail, because she is my voice. They are going to brainwash Sencontos and send him to Lucifer's Institution of Disobedience. They are planning to use him for the establishment of Antichrist's totalitarian government. They are also going to hang Respect, Dignity, and Honor. Then they are going to hire a very bad and evil man, called the False Prophet, who is the Priest of Death. He has the ability to deceive the whole world, but because of God's Great Grace, Elohim will not allow him to deceive the Elect of Jesus Christ. Secularia and Evolucy are atheists, but after the marriage, they will help the Antichrist to become their god. This is why they are trying so hard to get rid of the True Church, so that they can establish the Occult of Eternal Damnation. WHAT CAN YOU DO TO HELP ME? FOR WITHOUT THE FREEDOM THAT GOD ESTABLISHED THROUGH HIS SON JESUS CHRIST, YOU AND THIS NATION WILL PERISH! YOU WILL FALL INTO THE HANDS OF THE ANTICHRIST!

Let us pray! Oh, Lord God, in the infallible name of Jesus Christ of Nazareth, the Father of all, please hear us. We are about to go into that great prophesied war with the Ruler of Darkness. All of the people whose names are not written in the Lamb's Book of Life will side themselves with our archenemy. Your only begotten son, Jesus Christ, said that, "Thinkest thou that I cannot pray to my Father, and he shall presently give me more than twelve legions of angels?" Now, oh Great and Wonderful Elohim, we need them! Your servant — the least of all, less than the least, and the bottom of the bottom — cries out with the words of those who are under the altar, "How long?" Evil is increasing and righteousness is decreasing. The signs of the falling away are everywhere. The FREEDOM for the Church will soon cease for a short season. Tell us — who possess the name of Life — what to do. Reveal unto us the UNWRITTEN WORDS OF THE SEVEN THUNDERS THAT WE MIGHT UNDERSTAND. We thank you! We praise you! We honor you! We magnify your GREAT NAME! Not just ten thousand times, but ten trillion times time ten trillion times!

Come to my bedside, my dear brother, whom I love greatly, and who is my earthy defender and one of the guardians of the Truth. It is time for my departure. The poison that Secularia and

Evolucy injected into me is taking its toll! They are murderers in disguise! That beautiful flag, FOR WHICH I STAND, shall lose its meaning, because embedded in those sacred colors are the emblematical expressions of righteousness and justice! Even though it will be flying at half mast, the great light of it will be gone! Mr. Preambalo will shed a few tears, and Secularia and Evolucy will rejoice. My children, those still living, will cry and mourn sorrowfully for a very long time.

Bury me with my founding forefathers, George Washington, Abraham Lincoln, and those who died for me, and not with this wicked and adulterous generation! Sing my song that I love so much, which is "When I see Jesus, Amen."

I am beginning to bleed tears! My breaths are getting shorter! Lord God Almighty, thou seeth what those that hate have done. If they were of the seed of Adam, I would forgive them; but because they are of the seed of Cain, I cry out against them! Secularia and Evolucy have said in their hearts that I am old and not contemporaneous, and what they love is Totalitarianism. Lord God, give them the rewards of their works!

My brother, take good care of yourself! Secularia and Evolucy's next victim on Antichrist's hit list is the True Church!

Lord God Almighty, my spirit is now in your loving hands!

Freedom died on an undisclosed date, and was buried with those who loved and died for her.

Her epitaph on her foundational stone is "LORD HAVE MERCY ON MYSTERY BABYLON THE GREAT!"

Chapter Seven
God's Laws of Freedom

What is freedom? Is freedom the ability and opportunity to do whatsoever is emotionally pleasant to the mind and body without bringing harm to yourself and no one else? If this is the case, then slavery is the inability and the lack of opportunities to do that, which is emotionally pleasant to the mind and body. This analysis in conclusion, states that multitudes of people are unknowingly modern slaves. No soul on the face of the earth, who is living outside of God's Laws, is free. God sent the Christians to this country so that they could be free. Satan has incorporated his blinded servants into his occult to abolish our freedom.

Are the movie stars free? Millions and millions will say, "Absolutely, and I sincerely wish I was one." To show your shame and to commit yourself to fictional adultery and fornication for compensating riches is not freedom. Are the husbands and wives of those movie stars, who are married to them, happy with what they see? Maybe the money that they are making pacifies their spouse's conscious. Any man or woman who is in his or her right mind would not want their spouse pretending like they are making love to someone other than themselves. When the movie stars appear in their birthday clothes before millions of people, how can they be an example for their children and anyone else? They are not free, but have become the dominant slaves of Master Mammon.

Without God's Laws, this nation would have never existed. When God's Laws are completely removed from our judicial system, and the hearts of people, this nation will also cease to exist, as we know it. It will not be called the "land of the free," but the "land of enslaved totalitarian-influenced lawbreakers". When this act of lawlessness takes place, self-destruction will be standing at the doors of this great, sacred nation. I am trying my very best to tell you something that would cause you to open your eyes. The Antichrist has blinded you so greatly that you cannot understand that his hidden purpose is elimination. He has found a way to accomplish his objective. Please Mr. President, wake up! Do not let the voting of nine individuals bring this nation to shame! Is it right to vote on whether we need the Sun or not? The Ten Commandments is definitely not something that you vote on, because it is our lifeline for existence!

Are the drug dealers and their associates free? Do you really think that they actually want to kill and rob families of their joy and happiness for monetary gain? They would prefer selling ice cream peaceably and honestly, if they could generate the same amount of money. They would not be taking such a great risk of being caught or killed, if great worldly gain was not the main factor. Master Mammon has hired men and women to deal drugs, for one purpose only — which is to be his dominant slaves. The dominant slaves are employed to make and recruit peasant slaves. Master Mammon has written you a contract with microscopic laser printing at the bottom. It allegorically reads as follows:

To the individual who signs this contract: *You are hereby enslaved for life, with a big final payment* *in the lake of fire after you are deceased for all of the evil that you have helped us to perform. THANKS. We wish we could do more for you, but this is our best. The corporation is not allowed to tell you this, but we must put it in writing. If you (perchance) have a large microscope and discover these words, it will be too late. You have just sold your soul to the devil. There is no freedom for no one, who is on his or her way to hell.*

Are the nine blind judges free? Sure they are, because they are at liberty to do just about anything that seems right in the sight of the people. They have the authority to make major decisions for the people and to enforce their implementations. How can these judges be free after making the judgment to allow would-be children aborted out of existence? The river of blood from the holocaust of the unknown children has greatly stained their hands and mind. Whosoever is responsible for this catastrophe will never be free. The one and only way that they can be free is to repent.

Can you become an intricate part of the forces of evil and still be free? Are lied-to and brainwashed people free? There is no freedom in a lie or vain philosophy. Are the gays, lesbians, and prostitutes free? Are the women and men who expose their nudity for a living free? Can the gambling establishments that rob people of their hard-earned money be free? No individual who is a servant of wickedness, abominations, and sin will ever be free. When humanity turns from their wicked ways, then they will be free. Even though, the world population is increasing tremendously, the census for the Christians is decreasing, because of the apostasy.

There was a great day in the history of humanity when Elohim revealed himself before his elect. Not only did he manifest himself, but he gave to them the words of his Omniscient understanding of how to be free indeed. The summation of his words was for a threefold cause —for himself, his elect, and for the world. The present state that this world is in is because those same words that proceeded out of the mouth of God have been rejected time after time in history. When God's words were obeyed and honored, the people were free. When God's words were rejected, the people suffered greatly.

Each of the inhabitants of heaven obey and honor every word that comes from the mouth of Almighty God. That is the reason why there is an unspeakable joy and happiness in Elohim's presences. The only time that this peace and joy was broken in heaven was when Satan rebelled against God. Ever since that rebellion happened in heaven, there has been no continuous peace and joy on earth. How long do you think God will tolerate what is taking place, amongst the people, in this world? Will it be another decade or two? The prophetical signs are everywhere — which indicates that it will not be long.

Do people think that Elohim has abolished the words that he gave to his elect on Mount Sinai? The Ten Commandments is much more than just a great group of commands for his people. The Ten Commandments is also one of the greatest prophecies that ever existed. When God said, "I am the Lord thy God, and thou shalt have no other gods before me," he meant it. The people on earth now have many false gods, from every imaginable thing possible. After the great wrath of the Almighty God, there will never be another false god in existence.

The thousands of statues that man has made to bow before and worship will be cast down and destroyed. God said, "Thou shalt not make unto thee any graven image, or any likeness of any thing that is in heaven above, or that is in the earth beneath, or that is in the water under the earth. Thou shalt not bow thyself to them, nor serve them. For even one moment of time, do you think that the Almighty God did not ordain this from the time that he spoke these words throughout our entire existence? On the other hand, did he just ordain this commandment until the new dispensation of Grace was established? Oh ye men of so little understanding and knowledge, where is the wisdom that God ordained for you from the beginning? You have a deceived, corrupt mind. When you perceived in your minds to make that which Elohim said not to make, you became a part of illusive abominations. To justify the manmade sculptures of this day and age, church officials call them "word pictures." They conclude that God told Moses to make certain structures after his own design. It is true that the Ark of the Covenant has two cherubim made of gold after God's instruction. It is written, that Balaam said, "If Balak would give me his house full of silver and gold, I cannot go beyond the commandment of the Lord, to do good or bad of mine own mind, but what the Lord saith that will I speak." If this is the case, then how can the leaders in the churches think that they can justify what is taking place?

As the entire world can plainly see, you still have Romanic idolatrous, I must see, syndrome. Is this what you call Holy and intelligent? You just made that unspeakable, incapable, and as nothing- but-material thing a few days ago. Today, you are going to bow down before it and worship. Who or what are you worshipping? Jesus Christ of Nazareth said it plainly and undisputable. He told Satan, "It is written, thou shalt worship the Lord thy God, and him ONLY shalt thou serve. If Mother Mary were here in the flesh, it still would be an abomination before God to fall down and worship her. If the Apostle Peter were here, standing personally in Rome, it would be idolatrous to bow before him and worship. What would be your words when you bow to worship him? If Saint Peter could tell you FACE TO FACE a word, even now, he would tell you explicitly to stop AND HE WOULD PHYSICALLY STOP YOU FROM BOWING BEFORE HIM. Mother Mary would rebuke you to the highest degree that can come from a woman. She would be ashamed of you for your actions. She would let you know that heaven does not have a king and queen in authority, but only a king whose name is Jesus Christ of Nazareth, the only begotten son of the true and living God. The only one who God has allowed man to bow before other than himself is his only begotten son, Jesus Christ of Nazareth. Any other form of homage to anyone or thing is an abomination with no ifs, ands, or buts. The Apostle John fell down to worship before the signifying angel in the Book of Revelation. The angel said, "See thou do it not: for I am thy fellowservant, and of thy brethren the prophets, of them which keep the sayings of this book: worship God." When Paul and Barnabas were in Lystra, after they healed a crippled man, the people thought that the gods Jupiter and Mercurius had come down to them in the likeness of men. The people were in preparation to offer up sacrifices for them. But when Paul and Barnabas heard about what they were doing, they rent their clothes, and said, "Sirs, why do ye these things? We also are men of like passions with you, and preach unto you that ye should turn from these vanities unto the living God, which made heaven, and earth, and the sea, and all things that are therein: Who in times past suffered all nations to walk in their own ways. Nevertheless, he left not himself without witness, in that he did good and gave us rain from heaven, and fruitful seasons, and filling our hearts with food and gladness. Sirs, is it right in God's sight to let men and women bow before man made objects? Is it righteous to let men and women bow before you?" Those who have the gift of the Holy Spirit would never allow these things to take place in their lives, because they are free indeed, by the obedience of the Word of God.

God said, "Thou shalt not take the name of the Lord thy God in vain." Even though the pronunciation of the ineffable name of God is known by a few (if any), there must be an established honor and respect for the substitutions for his great name. There is no doubt in my mind with the anger and animosity present in this world that someone would try to use his ineffable name, which would bring chaotic damnable consequences on themselves. Vain people use vain words of idiotic vanity. When God's names (meaning all of them) are honored and respected, his mercy is readily available. TO YOU, YES, I MEAN YOU! Humble yourself in the sight of the Almighty God, and DO NOT LET ANOTHER FOUR-LETTERED WORD IN ANY LANGUAGE COME OUT OF YOUR

MOUTH! Respect God and his names and live, that you perchance my find grace in his sight unto salvation.

The evil words that now proceed out of the mouths of men and women will cease and be no more. The mouths from which they came will utterly be punished, unless they repent. The mouths from which these evil words came signify enslavement and bondage under our archenemy that is the devil. The mouths that refrain from speaking such evil words, are justifiable, free, and are not a part of totalitarianism.

Today is your birthday. Do you really want to work? Tomorrow is your wedding anniversary. Are you going out to dinner? You just ended your record-breaking harvest. Are you going to be thankful, eat, and rejoice? Jesus Christ of Nazareth has risen and the enmity that was between God and man is in remission. To those who understand, what are you going to do? You are going to glorify God fervently to the best of your ability. God finished his works in six omnisciently-known mathematical days. On the seventh day, which is called by God the Sabbath Day, he rested. The word rest, after God finished making all things, is not in reference of being tired and worn out, but means overwhelming celebration with rejoicing. God said, "Remember the Sabbath Day, to keep it Holy." In keeping the Sabbath Day, you are not only just resting but also are weekly being reminded of how great and how good and merciful God really is for making so many wonderful things for humanity. It is in God's will that man should have a hallowed day of rest. That is the reason why he used the word remember. After working for six consecutive days, anyone whose mind is functioning normally should have a sincere desire to rest his or her body. He also used the word keep, which means that what he has ordained is perpetual.

Did God abolish this commandment? Is it in the best interest of man that he becomes a workaholic with little or no rest? Have greed and substances brought man to near insanity? Can you eat a mountain of gold? How would a diamond the size of a watermelon taste? Master Mammon has deceived so many with the desire to please and satisfy the eyes to no profit. The mountain of gold is not evil, nor the if-you-can-find-it diamond the size of a watermelon. It is how you obtain such a great treasure that can make you become very evil. If there is no mercy in your oversight of laborers, then you are under the influence of Master Mammon. Legitimate businesses are for the well-being of humanity and not for modernized enslavement. Today, gold is a precious and rare metal; but in the days of the wrath of God, a glass of clean water will be more valuable than a mountain of pure gold.

Again, I sincerely ask you: Did God change the ordinances concerning the Sabbath Day? Nowhere and at any time, in the scriptures, did Elohim make changes for this day. It is written, and it shall come to pass, that from one new moon to another, and from one Sabbath to another, shall ALL FLESH come to worship before me, saith the Lord. Although, Christians all over the world recognize the first day of the week, in concordance with the resurrection, as the day that they should worship, the truth is that God is the creator of the Sabbath Day, and Jesus Christ is the Lord of it. Regardless of what people may try to change, the Son of God will always honor his Father. God has never had in his mind the thought of changing the Sabbath Day to honor the desires of man. Then the question before us is how did we get so far from God's ordinances concerning the Sabbath Day? The answer to that question is plain and simple. You can find the answer to this question in Satan's library. God did not send his only-begotten son into the world to change the Sabbath Day. This also is not the works of the Holy Spirit. No one in existence has the right to change what God loves. Furthermore, when our Lord and Savior Jesus Christ returns, he will reestablish the ordinances for the Sabbath Day that his Father created for humanity from the beginning.

Am I wrong for telling you the truth? The first day of the week is a great day for all of the Saints in existence. However, the evil part is that Satan wants to abolish the Sabbath Day from being observed at all. It is in his plans to make man forget that there is a day called the Sabbath Day. This sacred day is a part of our freedom. Honor, remember, and keep the words for this day that proceeded out of the mouth of Elohim.

God's Grace is sufficient for those who can not keep the Holy Sabbath Day because of humanitarian necessities. But to profane this holy day — by doing things for your own greed and pleasure — is unacceptable.

Out of the mouth of Elohim, proceeded great words of wisdom of how parents should govern their families. God said, "Honor thy father and thy mother: that thy days may be long upon the land which the Lord thy God giveth thee." This commandment was for peace, security, prosperity, longevity, disease-free years, healthy children, and above all things, for a nation that is completely devoted to Elohim, our Omnipotent God.

If the whole world would honor and practice this commandment, the prisons would be empty; the funeral directors could not get rich; there would be no drugs, nor drug dealers; the guns would get rusty; the policemen would be sightseers; the population would only increase through wedlock; the judges could rest; the mothers could teach their children instead of trying to perform the jobs of men; there would be no violence in the streets; the doctors would have short hours; the trauma centers for the wounded would have to close; the cries of the grieving mothers would not be heard because of their murdered children; the houses of prayer would be full; every street in the country would be declared safe; the insurance rates would decrease; the security businesses would have to find an alternate source to generate an income; the demons would leave because they would not have bodies to possess; and homosexuality would be nonexistent. Shall I continue to acknowledge the endless benefits of bestowing honor into every child who comes into this world?

When honor is instilled within a child, in their adulthood they will, in turn, instill honor within their children. This perpetual commandment, if obeyed by all humanity, will ensure that at no time, after God spoke, that any one would be without honor. Every soul would know how to give honor and to receive honor. That baby in someone's arms would be learning how to give honor to whom honor is due, which firstly is his or her parents. In that same baby's life, when he or she is in their old age, they would be receiving honor from someone else who has been taught respect and honor.

Stop, look, and ask yourselves this question: "Where is the respect and honor?" Do the parents teach it? If so, why do so many children still use four-letter words in almost every sentence? How can a fifteen-year-old teen mother teach her son or daughter respect and honor? How can the drug dealers teach their children respect and honor? How can the prostitutes teach their children respect and honor? The point that I am trying to make is that there is only a very little honor and respect left in the world.

Honor and respect are the stepping stones to God's great Grace. If the leaders of the world had enough respect and honor for each other, the Gates of Peace would open, and their consulting would be for peace and not war. This respect and honor that I am referring to is not necessarily from old age, but is from the mouths of a wise mother and a caring father who were taught the same way.

My heart is saddened and what shall I say? The windows, in many homes, look like the bars on jail cells that are for criminals. The children in the streets are the new wardens. The people must pay the security companies to live in their own personal prisons. The schools must have metal detectors at the doors. These statements do not apply to everyone, but are ever more increasing factors. Teach every child how to keep this first commandment with promise and be a witness of how the world would change for the better. THE WORLD IS NOW BRINGING FORTH CHILDREN FOR TOTALITARIANISM.

Elohim—to keep the five other commandments from becoming actable — established the first five commandments. These laws of prevention would ensure that the evil workings of Satan would have no place to be active. When these first five commandments are honored, respected, and practiced, the wrath of Almighty God is asleep. However, when they are not lived by, accordingly, Elohim sends consequential destruction.

While you are reading this book, everything that God has said for men, women, and children not to do is being practiced to the extremities, with no attempt or intent to stop whatsoever! In essence, the people are trying to figure out how they can be more evil. The great words of fear that came from the mouth of Elohim are being rejected for the words of the Antichrist. The commandment— thou shalt not kill — will never be abolished until every murderer has been judged, sentenced, and removed. All of the people who have murderous micro-demons, from the seeds of the serpent, will have no part, whatsoever, in God's kingdom. BY REPENTING AND GOD'S ACCEPTANCE THROUGH FAITH, AND HONORING THE ATONING BLOOD OF JESUS CHRIST OF NAZARETH ARE THE ONLY WAYS THAT ELOHIM GAVE TO THIS WORLD TO HAVE

MURDEROUS MICRO-DEMONS REMOVED FROM YOUR BODY. THE MURDEROUS MICRO-DEMONS GIVE PEOPLE THE INSTINCT AND THE DESIRE TO KILL, EVEN WITHOUT A CAUSE. This commandment, if not obeyed, will cause you to become one of the sons or daughters of Cain, who slew his brother and became the first known murderer. Again, there can be no freedom as long as the children of Cain remain in existence. Because of God's great Grace, he is the only one with the jurisdiction to remove these children from his kingdom. The mental attributes of humanity are too intuitional. It is in the divine will of God that every soul comes to repentance. God is omni-patient, and will give men and women every possible opportunity to repent of their sins.

Why did God say, "Thou shalt not commit adultery?" Adultery is one of the most devastating acts that can be performed against a family. Adultery, when committed, opens the doors to incompetent instability of the mind. If you have the will to commit adultery, then you are apt to break all of the other commandments as well. Adultery was committed by everyone that performed the act, before God, before he or she was born. Your eyes are only for the present, but

Elohim's eyes are omniscient and omnipresent. Vengeance is instituted, after adultery, within the heart of the wounded husband or wife. True forgiveness for such an act can only be done by the pure in heart. Adultery destabilizes the whole community and is not easily forgotten. Amongst humanity, once there is a beginning of adultery, it seems to never end. From the throne of Elohim and to every known part of that family, including friends, will feel the affects of planned adultery. Please take note that God was talking directly to his chosen elect.

What is the definition for adultery and the catastrophic results thereof? A man or woman who has lied before God, before his or her spouse, before the officiant, and before a company of witnesses (if married before a congregation) is part one of the definition for adultery. Part two is that you helped bring more immorality into the world, making you a licensed immoralist. The third part is how you were deceived by an appearance, making you, a victim of abhorred uncleanliness. The fourth part is that you lose your status of a lady or a gentleman; your diploma for righteousness is taken away; and the seal of trust that you use to have is with Satan. Satan will put his trust in you to continually commit the same act over and over again, until you are consumed by your own lust. The fifth part is the one that hurts the family the most. Your dignity, respect, and honor are revoked to the point of almost non-existence. The sixth part is for those who are of the body of Jesus Christ. When these acts are discovered amongst the Saints, fear becomes a stronghold and protective preventions are in place to try to keep such a thing from reoccurrence. The seventh part is the worst of all. A professed Saint, said to be filled with the gift of the Holy Spirit; questionably ordained to preach the Gospel; whose name is possibly in the Lamb's Book of Life; who takes upon himself the will to expose his shame before another woman; to defile his body; bring Holiness to shame; causing the belittlement of the office of a minister; having no regard for the great atonement of Jesus Christ made on Calvary; grieving the Holy Spirit; and allowing Satan to bring you down to as low as a piece of bread. The spiritual deaths, by strange men and women, will have no resurrection unto life without repentance.

Satan has monopolized the divorce industry. What I really mean is that secretive polygamy is the new and stealthily trend of men and women, especial for movie stars. The only difference between polygamy and secretive polygamy is that one man is married to a number of women at the same time, the other one just gets rid of one and goes to the next one with no intentional desire from the beginning to stay and remain married. This is not a polygamous country, so Satan has devised a scheme to have his way and still cause people to be accepted in our society.

It is written, "Therefore if any man be in Christ, he is a new creature: Old things are passed away; Behold all things are become new. And all things are of God, who hath reconciled us to himself by Jesus Christ." The new unwritten and accepted concept is that now you can be a circuit creature, which means that you can be a new creature for a certain period, and then resurrect the old man when ungodly and lustful desires are active. After the old man is finished, that same individual returns back to the new creature epic, where he or she can be renewed as many times as they so desire, preferably after each affair.

Oh man and oh woman, where are the senses that God gave you? You already have a clean and honorable spouse. You know you are extremely guilty and grossly filthy. What is the difference between your wife and the woman that you are having an affair? What difference is there between your husband and that man? To your shame, you are an intricate part of death. Adulteries are the destroyers of freedom. The current statistics for the number of divorces and affairs that are occurring in our country are in the millions. If millions of husbands and wives are committing adultery and millions are getting divorces, what can be the only analysis concerning these statistics of our nation? The answer is simple: national demoralization. All over the world, the status is the same. From my childhood to adulthood, the results of adulteries do the most harm to children. You should stop committing adultery right now, and be a part of the freedom that Elohim has ordained for this nation.

Why did God only use the word adultery for unlawful and sinful physical intimacy? The reason is that physical intimacy was only allowed between a man and his wife with no exceptions whatsoever amongst his chosen elect. The children of Israel received this commandment from God for the well-being of the entire nation. They knew the consequences of committing adultery, and took every precautionary measure to ensure the preservation of young, virginal women for marriage only.

Look now and behold the world where you are living. Almost everything around us is becoming an instrument for the destruction of purity. The whole world is coming down with the DEATH-MATING SYNDROME, a condition that the Antichrist has invented for consequential eternal damnation. There are only a few exceptions. To Satan, the Antichrist, and his destruction crew, this syndrome is a great tool for vengeful destruction, but to humanity, this is an epidemical disease that affects the reproductive organs to the point of uncontrollable desires. The children are being poisoned into adulthood before its time. Men and women are turning to anyone and anything that can satisfy their desires, with no respect or dignity at all. This DEATH MATING-SYNDROME is turning people into beastly mutants. They are raping and killing children for the fulfillment of their desires. The priests are becoming pedophiles because they are not allowed to marry. The pets must stand on guard if they can. The mothers are falling in love with their sons. The fathers are having their own daughters. Furthermore, the census for the lesbian and homosexual population has increased to an unheard of city size.

Where are the people for disease control? Where are the economists who work for the government? Do you realize the cost for allowing this syndrome to spread and not be quarantined? This syndrome is costing our government billions of dollars. Is there anyone left on the planet who cares about the current state that we are in and about to becoming? Are you in a race or rage to become the first to be called MYSTERY BABYLON THE GREAT, THE MOTHER OF HARLOTS, AND ABOMINATIONS OF THE EARTH? I have never heard of someone trying to destroy himself or herself to eliminate others but terrorists. The government and a multitude of accomplices are spending millions of dollars to help promote this syndrome. I sincerely ask you, "Why are you doing this to this sacred nation and what is your answer?" The allegorical answers to these questions are that abominations and sins can generate the most money, and who cares about the state of being sacred. We need MONEY AND LOTS OF IT! Oh, brainedwashed man, who will deliver you from this madness? Is money more valuable than Freedom? Is the Antichrist your new god, the god of IMMORALITY? He will biotech your minds to the state of self-destruction and devastating lawlessness. LET THE ANTICHRIST ROT IN HIS OWN WAYS. HE WILL NOT SEE THE FIRST DEATH, FOR HE WILL BE PUT INTO THE LAKE OF FIRE ALIVE! He is the biochemist who made these demonic strands that are being embedded into the DNA of our earthly genes. GOD DID NOT MAKE YOU A MUTANT FOR EVIL, BUT A LIVING SOUL FOR RIGHTEOUSNESS.

Go right now and summon all of the psycho biologists together. Maybe we can get some concrete answers. Sirs, what are the mental affects of nudity and sexually-enhanced apparel on the emotions of humanity and their intimate desires? Do conversations of intimacy generate desires? I hope that none of you are working for the pornography industries. I hope that none of you are working for Hollywood and the movie industries. I hope that none of you are lobbyists and activists for gay and lesbian rights. I hope that none of you are atheistic and of the occult of Scientology. I sincerely hope and pray that you are not a part of the Islamic extremists!

You are here for clarity and clarity only. If any you have the symptoms of the DEATH-MATING SYNDROME, please leave. The effect of your judgment concerning this matter will affect the whole world for better or worse!

Almost all of the apparel that is being made in the world has attraction with intimacy in mind. Do not be deceived: this attraction begins with children for its continuation. God ordained physical intimacy for marriage and the reproduction of those who are married; but Satan has devised a way to enhance intimacy to the point of being psychopathic with a twist of commonality. If the manufacturers would have modesty in mind, the world could save billions of dollars each year to be use for humanitarian reasons, and not on the useless and senselessly inhumane effects of clothing that promote death mating. For a man to see less of a woman makes him a better person. For a woman to show less of herself earns respect. A better man and a respected woman constitutes freedom. Death mating, in many cases, begin with the eyes. To the women who do not believe us, go and buy a dress with the kitchen doors closed (that is, below the knees), and without the split up to the living room. Take the fishing hooks off your body, and the war paint off your face; cast your cancer sticks into the garbage can; refuse to use profane language; tell the Antichrist that I AM NOT GOING TO BE YOUR FOOL ANYMORE! I AM A FREE AMERICAN, AND NOT ONE OF YOUR AGENTS FOR IMMORALITY; you will and can see the impact that you would have in this world. I need about one billion women to participate in this event. By becoming a participant, your reward maybe so great that Jesus Christ our Lord will be the only one, amongst humanity, who is the possessor and the administrator unto you for helping him destroy the works of the devil and in turn help save yourselves from the wrath of God. The men would not be stimulated into mental sin. The women would earn and hold their positions as highly respected ladies. On the other hand, if this trend continues, the destruction for immorality is imminent.

Mental sin is the beginning of physical sin. When sin is finished, it brings forth death. Even though the opportunities are not present because of the laws of openly violent approaches to be physically intimate with someone, the dress code sends the message of availability. When you have millions of women, young and old, sending the signals of availabilities for physical intimacy, how are the men going to react? Some are going to use the consent approach, the sweet-talking and flirting individual with the words of vice, and a murdered conscious. Some are going to lie through their teeth, saying "I am not married." The unlawful acts, according to God's Laws, are now lawful amongst humanity making it easier for the operations of death mating to spread. Some are going to be possessed with microdemons, which will stimulate a man to the point of raping and killing to fulfill his desires. Some are going to take advantage of age: the helpless children and the elderly. So many are going to get married just for one thing, and that is the 36/22/36. After a very short period, again the eyes are wanting, not for his own wife or the wife for her own husband but for someone on the other side of the fence, because of a laced envision of lust. Then there are those who are possessed with eight demons, which have no need to be stimulated by the enhancement of intimate apparel. These individuals will destroy themselves, men and women, and innocent children for the anticipation of being rewarded with seventy virgins in paradise. Little do they know that they will be mating with fire and brimstone.

There is only one antidote in existence that can stop the spreading of the Death-Mating Syndrome and eventually destroy it. This can only be accomplished through by the atoning blood of Jesus Christ, whom God gave for the salvation of this world. When you began to believe and obey the words of truth, which is the Word of God, you will change and your desires will be met in Holy Matrimony or strengthened for pure uninterrupted abstinence by the Holy Spirit.

If perchance that you are successful for a short season to have God's Laws removed from our judicial system, what laws have you to replace them? God's Laws said, "Thou shalt not steal; Thou shalt not bear false witness against thy neighbor; And thou shalt not covet thy neighbor's house, thy neighbor's wife, nor his manservant, nor his maidservant, nor his ox, nor his ass, nor anything that is thy neighbor's." In summation of nine of his laws, he spoke through his only begotten son Jesus Christ of Nazareth and said, " Thou shall love thy neighbor as thy self." So what will be the new secular laws that you will accept from the Antichrist? Will it be the new profit laws of making sure that you are not caught for being covetously greedy with no mercy for the poor? Will it be the new law for coveting your neighbor's wife, which states that intimacy is not adultery between two consenting adults? Sin without forgiveness has no end. Will it now be the new and excepted unlawful and abominable acts of gays and lesbians, who are — allegorically speaking — joined together in Demonic Saidlock? Secularism has no laws, because Satan is not a lawgiver but a lawbreaker. The peace that Elohim ordained for this world will cease for a time. Secularism will create chaos to a phenomenal proportion. Millions will die because of satanic secularism. All of Elohim's Laws will be dishonored. People will be worshipping themselves, and what they possess. There will be no peace on earth and goodwill toward humanity, in this country, until secularism is destroyed and God's Laws are honored above every other law that exists in our judicial system.

In conclusion of this chapter, I know from declaring the Truth that millions of minds, not souls, will become very angry with the one who wrote this chapter. Let me tell you the Truth! These words are not my words, but I received them from Elohim for life and not death. IT IS SO GREAT TO

BE ANGERED INTO REPENTANCE, BY THE LOVE OF GOD, FOR ETERNAL LIFE!

Chapter Eight
The Ignorance of Evolution

When man leaves his bounds that God has set for him, and enters into the mysteries of creationism, he becomes ignorant. How can one understand and measure the wonderful and supernatural things that were made by the Almighty God, unless he reveals it? Can you determine the size of my soul? Does the soul grow? Where is the tongue of the soul? How and when did it become connected with the body? It is very apparent that you and no one else amongst humanity can answer these questions. If you could, you probably would try to cut one out of a man and put it in a jar to be analyzed. You might even try to make some and sell them!

Whosoever has said "There is no God" is a FOOL! In addition, whosoever brought the theory of evolution into existence is worse than a fool is. Because man was not there in the beginning, when Elohim created the heavens and the earth, someone gave him a lie to proclaim. That great ignorant lie, which came from the greatest deceiving liar, is being branded in the minds of multitudes of people.

If you made a machine, for determining the age of something, the size of a big city, how can that mechanism measure itself? The substance used to make that device was already here. The components came from what you are trying to measure. It is called new because you just put it together. You did not and cannot make one atom of substance of the thing that you just called brand new. It is called old because man has seen it for a long time. If you cut down a two-thousand-year-old tree, and ground it up for a paper product, how old is that product that you just produced? Can the sea say to the river, "How old are you?" Alternatively, can the rocks say to the mountains, "I am older than you are?" Elohim do not mark his supernatural works with time, but with past finding out. You are just wasting your time. The earth is as old as it was yesterday, and as new as it is today. It appears to be natural, but its contents were supernaturally made. You are as incompetent as you were a day ago, and tomorrow you will be more ignorant, because you will never cease to say, "This all happened by itself."

Instead of digging in the rocks, you should be looking for those gases that you said came together and created a big bang. If you can find those same identical gases, you in your own words, would be able to make many new and wonderful things. Maybe you can, with your lied-to theory, bang immortality into existence. Those gases are so great, according to you, that they made themselves. Those gases, according to the evolutionist, can make a man who has a soul. I am telling you the secret is not in the rocks! They are just too hard. How can gases come together and make flesh that can be healed, and the blood wherein is life? Why do only your nails and hair have a continuous growth, and not your body after you reach a certain age? You really should not have a doctoral degree for believing and telling a lie of deception! You are an abecedarian in mathematics, because you do not understand that nothing plus nothing equals nothing!

The trillions of tons of matter, in the universe, are being carefully sustained in perfect order that no one can explain. Why do you want to believe a lie? If God allowed you to see and know the mysteries of his creation, you would not live to tell someone. Faith also would be abolished. You can see this divine order. However, if you tell the truth, you probably would not have a job. It is better to tell the truth than to be a liar for gain's sake. By the way, when are we going to get our gills? On the other hand, have we passed that stage already? The next stage must be the development of wings for flying.

The scientists have, for many years, tried to find something in existence that would elevate the theory of evolution into an absolute fact. However, after spending billions of dollars in research, it remains a lied-to theory. From Eternity to Eternity, the only way you will ever find the Truth is through the acceptance of Jesus Christ of Nazareth. There are so many mysteries of life on earth that man cannot find out. Nevertheless, it is in his heart to go places like Mars, only finding out that it has some of the same substances as earth.

The scientists are desperately trying to make people believed that you could take nothing and make an entire universe. The words being used, by them, sound as if they were there shaking Master Nothing's hand. In the ancient times, the people had enough understanding to know that Master Nothing and Miss All-by-itself did not make the universe, but chose something extra ordinary, and called it their god. Which group of people would you consider more intelligent?

Chapter Nine
The Day of Humbled Submission

Oh evil one, where are you? Come from out of your hiding place! Are you in a den or in the rocks of a mountain? Where are you, oh wicked deceiver, who also deceived the people with cunning arts of delusions and lying wonders? Have you both tried to escape into the heavens? The goats are about to be judged! Can you run from him that will sit upon the Throne of David? I though that you were so brave and courageous, but now I hear the sound of great trembling in my ears! Where is your so-called deified dragon that you caused the people to worship? Did he grow some new feathers after he was thrown out of heaven like lightning? Look now, see, and behold the angel with the great chain in his hand and the key to the bottomless pit, who is the contractor with the seal, to bind, to shut up, and to seal Satan for a thousand years. As for you and your associate, you will be taking the exit ramp pass the bottomless pit and hell, directly into the Lake of Fire for all of your wicked and evil ways. There will be no funeral directors, nor grave sights needed, because of the nature of your sins and abominations. You will be exempt from death because of so much death and destruction that you brought upon humanity. You will be cast ALIVE into the Lake of Fire, and sentenced there without parole.

Howl all ye unrighteous ruling dignitaries of the earth! Your replacements have arrived! Put down your weapons and live! The son of the Great Creator is here! Listen to him and humble yourselves! His name is the Word of God. If you decide in your hearts to fight against him, you will be consumed without mercy! Call for an international conference and seek for the wisdom of the Truth and of the aged. Read the words of the prophets of the Holy Bible aloud to everyone on earth! Use the media, without limitations, for salvation from destruction. Lay hold of those two great deceivers and hold them fast!

Be not one of those who will become a meal for the fowls of the air. To the deceived who preside at Rome: what are you going to do? Will there be a continuation of what is now taking place in your congregations and amongst yourselves? Will Jesus Christ of Nazareth accept the dogmatism that you have established for the people over hundreds of years? To the deceived Nations of Islam, what are your words and who are now the infidels? Lo and behold, your forefather Abraham. Will the people who believed and trusted in Mohammed be worthy to sit down in peace with their forefather, or will he rebuke you greatly for your unbelief in Jesus Christ of Nazareth?

Hear now the great cries in that great city, Mystery Babylon, that shall be no more, because of her fitly name! Who is responsible for her fall? Are you one of those who are responsible? What is her present name and where is her place? Did you — yes I mean you — commit some of the sins and abominations that gave her the name of the Mother of Harlots and Abominations of the earth? It is very apparent that the place on earth where the sins and abominations of the people are the greatest, which influenced the whole world, is the place, and this needs no philosophical analysis.

Where are the scientists who said that there is no God? Stop your wailing for it is in vain! Not only did you lie to the whole world, but promoted it to the highest degree and denied the truth. Shall God's great Grace help you? Why should the precious blood of Jesus Christ of Nazareth now be atonement for you? Are you that ignorant to think that after going to school and obtaining a doctorial degree in evolution, to teach the world that there is no God, you would be worthy of forgiveness? You, the evolutionists, helped the Antichrist to become falsely deified. After you were deceived from being atheistic, you helped him!

All of you, who attend worshipping services, who are drunk with the wine of entertainment, wake up and be sober! Why have you shown the fervent desire for music and singing more than for the Word of God? Is it the monetary gain, or is it that God's House is a place for justification? When the leader of a congregation allows rappers, break dancing, ballet performances, and comedians into God's sacred and anointed services instead of prayer, supplications, singing of hymns, and above all, the preaching of the unadulterated Word of God, that man is drunk with the wine of entertainment! There is no salvation in the deceitful operations of being entertained? YOU NEED SALVATION THROUGH JESUS CHRIST OF NAZARETH! Music and songs are not the foundation of our right back to the Tree of Life. Worshipping God in the beauty of Holiness is not for your amusement and emotional gratifications. Are you a part of that glorious church without a spot or wrinkle, or any such thing? Will this contemporaneity be accepted into the Kingdom of Heaven? Will the angels and the saints of God in heaven adopt what now is taking place in God's House? YOU ARE SO DRUNK OFF DRINKING DEMON ALE NUMBER 7! Humble yourself immediately, because in a few days, the entertainment will cease and true worshipping will be restored!

The prophesies in the scriptures have declared that the earth will shake, and the cities will fall. A certain city will be divided into three parts because of this earthquake. The earth will be sanctified and be ridden of many evils in its existence before its maker arrives. Are you one of the inhabitants of this city called Babylon the

Great? You need to do some intensive research, prayer, and repenting if you do not know. Your discoveries may be your key to salvation.

Where are you, PlayWho, and the rest of you, who are made rich from shame, sin, and abominations? What are you going to do HollyStick for Emanuel is here? I heard that there would be no more you-know-what in the City! What will the talk show hosts and hostesses do, for the showing, the proclaiming, and the entertainment of people with the works of the devil will come to an end? The Lord of Holiness is here, and he will thoroughly cleanse his Father's Footstool! The designers of SexWear and AttentionWear will be out of business. The garments of holiness will be the attire for the inhabitants of the Kingdom of Heaven. Men will look like Holy men, and the women will look like Holy women, distinctively. The Kingdom of Heaven will have no need for supermodels! The apparel of Elohim will be the new attire for the Saints.

To the possessors of mass destructive weapons: wake up, for that same man who changed water into wine is here! He has the ability to change uranium into sugar, and the power to heal and remove the woes of biological warfare with the words of his mouth! It has been made known in the scriptures that all power that is in heaven and in earth is in the hand of Jesus Christ of Nazareth. HUMBLE YOURSELVES AND LIVE! Even though the Battle of Armageddon is imminent, some of you can escape the consequences of obliteration that will take place upon those who think, in their hearts, that they can destroy the King of Kings! DO NOT LET THE ANTICHRIST PERSUADE YOU THAT YOU CAN!

Ye angels, hear now the words from the Word of God! Gather together all of the drug dealers, and their accomplices from the four corners of the earth. Find the pimps and their prostituting associates and bring them to the judgment! Bring the gang leaders and their members, for there will be no one who offends the King of Kings in his kingdom! Everyone who is a part of iniquity must stand before the judgment seat of Christ! God's kingdom will be free of occults, false prophets, and all who are part of them! What are you going to do, gamblers and its establishment owners, when the number of your days have come to an end? The camps of nudity will be no more! The rappers of filth, the dancers of fornication, the players of demonic music, and all things that are alike are removed out of the Kingdom of Heaven! Bring the abortionist and the merciless mothers that have not repented here, for they shall not escape this judgment! Behold, the liar's judgment is also at hand!

Wake up Freedom and be Free Indeed! Your enemies — the Antichrist and the False Prophet — are in the prison of the second death. Your Lord and my Savior is here! The tables are set and the Feast of A Thousand Years has begun! Rejoice, for all of those who are of the evil one are absent! Take your places ye well-done servants and rule with the Lord according to his word. The spoils of the earth are our inheritance, and the reward for humility and obedience. The poor shall be rich in the Lord and shall never want anymore! The winds of destruction shall be at peace! The earth will shake no more for she shall be clean! The mountains of fire shall humble themselves and rest! Wars and rumors of wars your funeral is today, because the Prince of Peace is here. Gather the whole population of the merciless terrorists that the Lord may judge them and give them the reaping of what they have sown in the earth! The unlawful, demonized judges who legalized the slaughtering of Elohim's children must stand before our just Judge and be judged! The judges who made the ordinances to pollute the nations with sodomists shall never again be at rest!

Come now, oh unspeakable joy, and manifest yourself! Let the world know that the Lord is in his Holy Sabbath and we are exceedingly glad to praise his Holy name. Our thoughts are pure and holy, and our ways righteous. The commandments of the Lord are free to be upheld. The council of the people is for good, and we will not make the Lord to grieve in his holy temple!

Chapter Ten
Ruled By Psychic Holograms and Telepathic Communications

In the beginning of Pride — when Jealousy, Envy, and the knowledge to exalt self came together and entered into a certain archangel named Lucifer — there was a great rebellious revolution in Heaven. Pride used to be just a word without a person, but it was manifested when Lucifer decided to be tantamount with Elohim. The essence of Pride is to be deified and exalted above all. Every soul who thinks that he or she is above all others is born of Pride. All of the evil works that ever existed are the offspring of Pride. For thousands of years, Pride — which is the greatest enemy of Love — has made know its deeds through rebellious Lucifer.

Everyone who possesses the gift of Pride has a ruler. The gift of Pride is the disease called Never Enough and Greater Than Thou. Without a name in the Lamb's Book of Life, you will be under the authority of the one who possesses Pride until death. When you are of an age of accountability, and your name is on the Second Death list, you will be ruled through holograms and telepathic communications. You will have the insane ability to accept and practice the words of what is being communicated to you. The instructions for every evil deed begin with the communications between Pride and his associates, and the corrupted accepter. After being instructed and deceived, the manifestations began to exist.

An adulterer's first instruction is to make sure that he is not caught. Even though he has a clean and respectable wife, the telepathic expressions are to inform the deceived that the feeling, face, and body of that other woman will be better than his own will. Pride will never tell you that you are destroying your soul! To intensify the desire into an act, psychic holograms are shown. These holograms of the imagination are the ones most frequently used. Occasionally, Pride goes to the extreme depth and produces a hologram in a dream of the futuristic act of the intended prideful sin. Pride will not let you know that you were caught before you were born!

The means of receiving psychic holograms and telepathic communications into the mind are supernatural. There are no plugs that you can disconnect or wires that you can cut that can stop these kinds of communications. Only the Saints of the Highest God have the ability, through Jesus Christ our Lord, to reject evil holograms and evil telepathic expressions that come from Pride and his associates.

In order to reject evil, you must have the knowledge of what is right. Without the knowledge of what is right, from the Lord of Righteousness, the nature of the poison that is in us will take its course. Very soon, all excuses for being unrighteous will be eliminated. The Preacher of the Air will declare the Truth of Righteousness, which is the everlasting Gospel, to the whole world. No nation will be able to say, "I have never heard the True Gospel of Jesus Christ!"

The earth is now polluted to an extreme state of manifested words of Pride. It is so polluted, it is being classified as a commonality. Pride is voicing us into the woes of destruction! Pride said, "Kill your offspring," and millions of mothers did it! Pride said, "You can exclude gender from marriages," and thousands agreed. Pride governs the judges who pass laws against righteousness. Pride rules the lives of homosexuals and lesbians. Pride has complete control of the minds of terrorists, if God does not intervene.

The perfect words of the excellent example of the communication between Pride and a person are written in the Holy Bible. This example is for the Saints of God. When Jesus Christ of Nazareth was in the wilderness, to be tempted by the devil, he never yielded to one word that proceeded out of the mouth of our archenemy. Even thought the power was present to perform every act (because of being omnipotent), he never was submissive at any time. Hungry through the flesh, the response was in God's Word. Being tempted to tempt his Father, again the answer was from the Holy Scriptures. The last group of words that came from the mouth of Pride was for the death of the whole church. Without the Most Holy Sacred Sacrifice of Atonement, the enmity between God and man could not be healed. The supernatural, psychic holograms of the kingdoms of the world never had any affect whatsoever upon the mission of Great Grace and Divine Salvation. Oh ye Saints of God, you must do likewise with all of thy might.

The examples of yielding to Pride are also written in the Word of God. The offer to Eve to be greater than her present state was accepted. The offer to Cain to kill his brother Abel — for the removal of his brother's works that was more pleasing to God — was accepted.

Every word that proceeds out of the mouth of Pride is a part of a lie or for deception. If there is a fulfillment, it is the truth unto death and destruction. When King David saw Bathsheba's body, which was the property of Uriah, he allowed Pride to enter into all of his senses! Pride made him forget the Laws of God and its consequences for breaking them. The lust of the flesh, through his eyes, started a truthful reaction unto a consequential death sentence. He forgot about all of the wives and concubines given to him by God and he began to covet for more. Pride exalted him above the obedience of the Law and the righteousness of salvation, and in essence brought him down to Hell if he did not repent. When the fulfillment of Pride was finished with David, the seed of his sin blossomed, and

Bath-sheba was with child. Again, Pride entered into all of his senses even greater than before. Pride exalted him to be the supreme judge of life and death. David's first reaction under the influence of Pride was to create a lie by having Uriah plant a seed that he thought would be his own. When the persuasive notion to leave his dedicated post to have his own wife did not work, Pride gave him the instructions on how to destroy Uriah, make Bath-sheba a widow, then marry her, and be innocent before the people with his offspring. However, through the knowledge of Our Omniscient God, his works of Pride was known before he was born. God's Grace, that was for the New Covenant, was granted to King David and he lived his course and repented.

Pride has clothed himself with the garments of the innocent. He stands before the congregation in white and deceives the people. The stains of sodomy are hidden in the night of his covering. He executes the office of a priest and performs the Eucharist out of fear, not knowing that he stands in the shadow of death. Pride has a doctoral degree to aid humanity in its sickness and to be a comforter at the time of death. Hidden under his purified uniform and sterilized name is a genocidal butcher of Elohim's children. The aneurisms of death are upon him. The Truth will unveil the hidden deeds of Pride to the world.

Chapter Eleven
One of the Last and Final Pleas To Repent

The time in which you should not harden your heart is ending, and tomorrow is a day that no one wants to see without repentance. "Then, come now and let us reason together," saith the Lord shall soon be no more! The sickle of God's wrath is in his hand and time shall soon be no longer. Shall I plea to God for all of the souls who will not listen, even though they dig their own graves with committing so much sin? The day of God's Great Grace has an end.

The day will come when someone will say that "The Lord has ended his patience, and he has forgiven enough. Again the Lord of Host is grieved, but not to utterly destroy, but to judge." Come now to the market place of the judgment of the Lord that you may exchange your sins and abominations for your rewards! Since you love the taste of sin, you will not enjoy the left over of it. Shall God's Grace continue and his wrath stay in its rest while you are determined to cover the earth with evil? The spots are cities and the wrinkles are as the waves of the sea. Is there any hope left for you in the well of salvation? The blood of your ignorance is everywhere, killing without a cause. Will Elohim speak to you before the judgments began, or have you perceived that there will be none? Are the words of your heart that of a fool?

Ye do not have a just law to sin, but you glory in your abominations. The destructions of the past are not learned, and as soon as the chastening of the Lord has ceased, ye fall into being worse! You ask for God's blessings, but will not repent! When he does bless, you forsake all of my ways. How can you receive good when the room is full of evil? Your rivers are bloody, and your streets are filthy. You have proclaimed a day of prayer, but without repentance. First, repent then pray lest it is in vain. Did you rebuke the sodomites and the butchers of Elohim's children? Did you restore the Commandments of Freedom and Life? What did you do that his wrath be turned away? Show God your goodness and the signs of your repentance! When you are well, you set forth your hand to destroy righteousness! When you are sick, your desire is to pray. After Elohim heal, you raise your hand again to corruption. Is the Lord of Pity guilty for being righteous, and are you innocent for being evil? Shall the All-Seeing Eye of God hide himself in the heavens, and allow you to destroy the wonderful things that he has made?

The footstool of Elohim is a place of manifestation, and a room of determination. It is not a house for the Omniscient God of All to determine whether you are good or evil, for he knows all things, but to be a witness to every soul of what and who you really are.

Will the Lord say more than what he has already said? You have 6000 years and more of the knowledge and workings of the Lord, our God. He gave this world prophets and those who witnessed the words of truth with every generation. He did not spare his own son, but gave him up to be sacrificed for all. Now, after all that Elohim has done, the people still want to serve and obey the creature. Why is it that you love death more than life?

The Word of God in the books has made it known to this generation that there will be a time and a people who will not repent. Even though the Lord will chasten greatly during that time, they will not listen nor repent. Accordingly, to the wisdom that I have received from the Spirit of Truth, through Jesus Christ our Lord, I have perceived that this is that generation.

Lord God Almighty, in the name of Jesus Christ of Nazareth, the owner of everything that is in existence, please hear thy servant's prayer. Grant me the opportunity that I may be heard through thy only begotten Son. I am nothing of myself and never can be. There are those now present in the world who love you and are fervent in it. We need help from thy Holy Hill. Who is right amongst men besides our Lord and Savior? Every soul is in debt to thy Great Grace. The falling away has begun, and the man of sin will soon be at liberty to destroy and deceive. Please, Oh Most Holy Father, do not let thy servant live to be deceived or to bring shame to thy Holy Name. I am so unworthy that I can only ask you from the Throne of Grace. I am not consumed because the Blood of Atonement is present. I am asking you for the Promise of Life. Whatsoever is needed and what I must do to be the least of all in thy kingdom, please show me. Number my days to today, if it will be a part of the fulfillment of thy promise. I have been in a pit before and have no desire whatsoever to return to it. It is better to live a short holy life than a long life unto death. The operations of deceptions are everywhere, and the resistance from the Saints are of little significance.

Chapter Twelve
The Thirty-Fourth Degree Of Melt Down

All of the brethren of the Fellowship and all of the sisters of the Sisterhood, please hear my voice! Elohim will soon use his gavel to call this world into the Order of Divine Judgments. When this happens, the whole world will hear the sound of it and be terrified. On that day, Faith will rest and Absolute will be manifested. When the Truth and the Life shall appear, every eye shall be a witness of him. After heaven declares his presence, the Rite of Holiness for this world will begin.

My concern is that there are many of you who have not accepted Jesus Christ of Nazareth as your Lord, Master, and Savior. This chapter is a petition for your well-being. The speculative foundational skills of Freemasonry and of the Order of the Eastern Star have their basis from the Holy Bible. You know right well that you are not without the knowledge of Salvation. Both orders have a great decision to make. You need to act now, because time is of the essence. There are many changes that are taking place in our world, and it is not for the good of mankind!

There is a new order on the horizon, which is being voiced as the New World Order. The signs of this order are maturing into existence little by little. Satan has devised a way to hide his evil works behind pleasant words. The New World Order is really the Order of Totalitarianism under the jurisdiction of the Beast called the Antichrist. Without the Seal of Elohim, you will be vulnerable to the state of becoming a part of this order. The earthly wisdom and knowledge of the degrees of Freemasonry cannot keep the Beast from making you a part of the Order of Totalitarianism. You must be sealed by Elohim with the Holy Spirit to be sure of being protected.

Every one of you has an opportunity to be delivered from being marked for death by the Antichrist. If you have decided to be deceived unto damnation, then this chapter is not for you but for those who have been elected for hope unto Salvation. The time of recruitment for consolidating everything under the Order of Totalitarianism has begun. The Antichrist, through the False Prophet, will deceive every one of you whose name is not in the Lamb's Book of Life. The allotment of seven years, in the Testament of God's Creation, will be fulfilled by the Antichrist.

After the order of this manifested dispensation, which is the disclosure of the works of man under the New Covenant, the Thirty-Fourth Degree of Meltdown will begin. Can any one of you say, "We will not have anything to do with this degree?" Please brace yourself for the words of Truth! Who are you, oh little one? Do you have a will that you think that you can bring into existence? Where is your power? Don't you know that all power that is in heaven and earth was given unto the Son of Elohim? It is by God's Grace that you were allowed to become a Freemason or an Eastern Star. You do not possess the power of Life. How then can you perceive that you will not be a part of what is about to take place? Sound the gavel and call to order the council, because after the Order of Totalitarianism has fulfilled its days, the meltdown of all meltdowns will begin. No man, woman, creature, power, principality, or angel shall be able to prevent the beginning and the end of this degree from existing!

After the fulfillment of the prophecy of the Abomination of Desolation, every thing, every one, every place, every nation, every government, and in summation every part of creation that is not of God will be destroyed or reconstructed to be a part of that glorious Kingdom of Heaven. If you are an accepted part of the Kingdom of Heaven, you will be blessed to continue. Nevertheless, if you are not a part of the Rite of Holiness, and in the past, your works were offensive; Freemasonry and every other order will end.

To all of those whom Elohim has sealed, please listen very carefully. Elohim sealed you with the Holy Spirit for entering into his blessed kingdom. Because of the renewing of the mind, the Antichrist cannot have an affect on your soul. When the Antichrist incorporates the kingdoms of this world under his jurisdiction, you cannot and must not be a part of anything that is against the Will of God.

Can words and signs change the mind of the Almighty? Can the initiations make you right? Will the numbers of you constitute a continuation of this order? Will the knowledge that you possess save you? If all of these things would be justified as righteous and the means to enter into the Kingdom of Heaven, then why did Elohim send his Son into the world to die for us all? The Rite of Holiness is the life that you live unto God after being converted. Sin and abominations are not a part of this rite. The knowledge and wisdom of salvation is incomplete without its application.

What then shall I say? Shall I become a part of you? The secrets and mysteries of Elohim are in Holiness. The angels of God are present to help and assist those who are a part of Holiness. Another brother can only help and assist his brother in the natural order, but in Holiness, Elohim, Jesus Christ, the Holy Spirit, and the supernatural host of heaven are present in the time of trouble. All of you should live a life unto God for deliverance from the woes of death.

Sirs, how can you be free, if you are under the bondage of sin? How can you resist the Grace of God that he ordained for you through his son Jesus Christ? Is it because some of you are against Christ? In the Mysteries of the Thirty-Fourth Degree, those who are against Jesus Christ of Nazareth will be made manifested. In the Rite of Holiness, Jesus Christ of Nazareth bears the two-edged Sword of Truth in his mouth. Everyone who lived the sounds of Holiness will enter into his kingdom. Everyone who has been marked with the expressions of sin shall be cast out!

I am praying to the Lord our God that you stop searching for more Light and give you the understanding that the Light has already come. The Light that is in Holiness is the greatest Light, wherein there is no darkness at all. The only initiation that is needed is the water baptism in the name of Jesus Christ of Nazareth, and the will of the mind to repent. Elohim will perform the Act of Regeneration, through by the Holy Ghost.

Brothers of the Brethren, and Sisters of the Sisterhood, will you be there when the Secrets of Faith shall be revealed? Will you be there when the Mystery of Elohim shall be made manifested? Will you be there when Charity shall rest upon every soul? In order to fulfill the "I will be there" you must fulfill the "How to be there." Moreover, the only how to be there is through Jesus Christ our Lord. Amen.

Conclusion

Cast dusts upon your heads, all ye alienated untouchables, for the Savior of this world will take away the UN- part of you! The words of your evil, inhumane liberties that proceeded out of your mouths and went into perdition will soon be cut off! The liberties of righteousness and justice shall be manifested throughout the remnant of the people. The trouble that you are in is past the scope of forgiveness. Civil liberties have restrictions and limitations, and they were never ordained for evil motives. You went beyond the bounds of God's will and granted Satan and his evil host of darkness destructive liberties. God threw him out of Heaven and now you have taken Satan in for our destruction! Not only did you take him in, but also those who were thrown out with him. After you took him in, you made him your chairman. Without a shadow of doubt, he is going to turn against you! His nature is as a Black Widow. When this nation falls into the hand of the Antichrist, you will be the prime agent for the cause of the enactment of his totalitarian government. You are the ones who promoted the liberties of the desecration of our sacred democracy.

To the Commander in Chief, this league is the catalyst to make our military forces weak. How can you fight a war with women and inordinate intimate individuals? Will God help you when you pray to him in the time of war? Certain civil liberties are out of bounds when it comes to the survival of our sacred nation. How can you pray to Elohim for guidance, when you have allowed the desecration of prayer in the public places, allowed the abortionist to kill his children, and allowed the passing of laws to promote sodomizing? God will only help you and this nation when they repent of all of its evil ways! To be honest with you, the wrath of Jehovah-Nissi is upon us for the non-compliance of his Divine will.

Are we now the merciless puppets of this league of antichrists? From the beginning unto this very day, sodomy has always been an act of abomination! Before the Ten Commandments were given, it was evil. Before Jesus Christ of Nazareth came into this world, it was evil. Before the Constitution of the United States of America was written, it was evil. After thousands of years of being evil, how can it now be right! Where did the word sodomy come from? Was there a city called Sodom? Did Elohim destroy that city? The lessons of the past have no effect upon those who are possessed with micro-demons! Sodomy destroys the vital characteristics of masculinity, which is needed in the time of war to defend this great nation. Sodomy, which is the manifested presence of micro-demons, gives men the characteristics of femininity. FEMININITY AND WAR IS A VERY BAD MIXTURE, IN WHICH WAR ALWAYS WINS.

How can a healthy mother, with a healthy fetus, decide in her heart to destroy the Gift of Life that God has given to a boy or girl? If there was an instigator involved in the decision making, then it is premeditated murder! Woe woe woe unto the ones who yielded, and allowed the enactment of the Death Rite of Innocent Blood of one or more of Elohim's children to take place. The first woe is because the evil-minded mother was merciless and did not understand that her mother was merciful. The second woe is because you allowed someone else to destroy a great part of you without a just cause. The third woe is because you profane the statues of a civilized family, a devoted mother, a human being, and for allowing this act to take place before our Omnipresent God, who is the Father of all. The only way that you can escape the pending woes is through confession and essentializing repentance.

Is there a court upon the face of the earth where I may plea my case? If there is one, please tell me because the courts that I know of are under the influence of Totalitarianism! The just judges are rebuked and are now without pay. What must we do that our children be not consumed? I will take my case to the Truth Court where the Truth is disclosed and all lies are brought to silence.

When the children prayed, babies weren't having babies! The citizenship burdensome cost for incest, rape, and illegitimacy is $126,000,000,000.00 dollars over a course of eighteen years for 1,000,000 illegitimate children. If the children had prayed, the prison industry would have never reached the capacity that it is at today. The citizenship burdensome cost for prisons, court cases, lawyer fees, and security is $1,000,000,000,000.00 over a period of twenty years for about 1,000,000 inmates! When the children prayed, they learned how to be ladies and gentlemen, and not murderers and robbers who have little or no reasoning. The pain, grief, and suffering — caused by children who became vicious criminals — are present in almost every city. Your education is incomplete without the knowledge of how to please God, and how to offer up a sincere prayer to him. When the children prayed and had devotional services, the schools were safe and without metal detectors. The burdensome cost for security, to the taxpayers, is $25,000,000.00 for personnel and detection devices per 1,000 schools for ONE YEAR! When the children prayed, the populations of drug-selling, drug-using, and infiltrating street gangs were very insignificant. The burdensome cost to the taxpayers of today for hospitalization, rehabilitation, counseling, funeral arrangements, treatment of hyperactive children, and medications, is about the sum of $400,000,000,000 every 20 years. When the children stopped praying, many of them became gays and lesbians. The great and burdensome cost to the people of this nation is the lost of ONE NATION UNDER GOD.

When the people offered up fervent prayer to Elohim, and repented, he heard them, came to their rescue in the time of trouble, and delivered them. This league is determined to remove one of the most important forms of communication in existences, which are the prayers of the righteous to Elohim. Satan has come up with a devious plan to excommunicate children from hope unto eternal damnation. They will eventually become the Antichrist's recruited adults unless the people repent, seek God, pray, and intervene for them. Satan is putting forth his greatest effort on how to destroy the minds of our children. They are the most vulnerable ones of our society.

Where are the military generals who have understanding? Do you think that Satan is going to manifest the Antichrist, who will sit in the temple at Jerusalem, with an ever-present and powerful nation breathing down his neck? The beginning of the war, before the Battle of Armageddon, is mind-conquering with no physical weapons involved. Are we going to sit still and watch the antichrists take over our country? Or are we going to fight against them with the Sword of the Spirit?

Sirs, you are being undermined by the Antichrist's six-star generals. Look at the destruction that has taken place from desecration, reasoning failure (and many other nonviolent tactics) from the minds of them. The False Prophet haven't even open his mouth publicly yet, and still there are many mental manifested defeats! Sirs, stop listening to the evil propaganda that has proceeded from out of the mouths of the evolutionists and secularists, and start praying for deliverance from this evil!

How many years are we from the war, in which Jerusalem will be taken into captivity? The mental part is now in motion! Someone needs to make a major country-saving decision. Will this country be a friend or foe? Whether you understand it or not, I firmly believe that Satan has conducted a capability study of the potentiality of our armed forces for the futuristic strategies, that will take place in the war to take Jerusalem. I hate to say this, but the Truth is the Truth. Jerusalem is going to fall into the hands of the Antichrist for three-and-a-half years. What does this mean for this country? It means that we will help the Antichrist or be defeated by him! I PERSONALLY WOULD RATHER BE DEFEATED FOR THE LOVE OF GOD AND

HIS PEOPLE, THAN TO BE DEFEATED UNTO DEATH IN THE BATTLE OF ARMAGEDDON THAT WILL TAKE PLACE THEREAFTER!

The manifestations of mind-conquering are everywhere. How many minds in the world do you think that Satan has conquered over the past twenty years? How many Saints are now present in the world? Is the number of minds that are being conquered increasing or decreasing? If there is an increase, then the number of Saints is decreasing. When the increase of mind conquering is full enough for Antichrist's totalitarian government, he will come forth and manifest himself. He will hide himself until the Apostasy has completed its course. If Satan had the ability to conquer the minds of one third of God's angelic host, then what about the minds of men that were made a little lower than them? HAS SATAN CONQUERED YOUR MIND? If you are not or will not become a repented Saint, then your mind has or will be conquered by him. Am I telling you the Truth? OPEN UP YOUR EYES THAT YOU MAY SEE FOR YOURSELF OR KEEP THEM CLOSED TO BE A WITNESS IN THE FUTURE OF THE DESTRUCTION OF MIND-CONQUERING.

It is the blessed, civilized, working families that contribute the most revenue, through taxes, for the well-being of this nation. The new Nuclear families will soon bring this nation to a chaotic shame without repentance! A house full of sin will eventually fall. Because of righteousness and prayer, this country has been so greatly blessed. But because of iniquities, sins, and abominations, our eyes are witnessing catastrophic destruction.

THE VICTIMS WHO HAS ACCRUED LOSSES FROM THE PROMOTION OF THESE EVIL AND INHUMANE LIBERTIES FROM THIS LEAGUE, BY LAW, MUST RECEIVE COMPENSATION. I AM LOOKING FORWARD TO MEETING YOU IN THE TRUTH COURT OF JESUS CHRIST.

To the mothers and fathers of human dignity, IF YOU HOLD YOUR PEACE AND ALLOW THE COURTS AND THIS LEAGUE TO DESECRATE THE RIGHTEOUSNESS OF THIS GREAT NATION — THAT WAS GIVEN TO US THROUGH JESUS CHRIST OUR LORD, BY OUR FOUNDING FOREFATHERS — YOUR CHILDREN WILL GROW UP TO BECOME THE ETERNAL INHABITANTS OF THE LAKE OF FIRE.

About the receiver from the Author of Grace

It is appropriate to declare to the world the Truth. Man and all of the wonderful works thereof is a precious gift from Elohim our Father. If I would take the credit for this work, I would not be telling you the Truth. I will make a boast in the LORD our God for the wisdom he has given me to proclaim the Truth. This gift of wisdom, to manifest the Truth, came through the Doors of Righteousness and did not come through an educated nor intuitional mind. The end of every lie is at hand, and the Truth concerning those lies is about to be disclosed.

www.ingramcontent.com/pod-product-compliance
Lightning Source LLC
Chambersburg PA
CBHW020246290526
45784CB00003B/1116